Dolor del Dólar –

A Financial
or a Cultural Crisis?

by Mónica Oliva

This is a translation by Graham B. Rickett (Stroud, U.K.) of the original Spanish version of El Dolor del Dólar, Editorial Dorothea, 2011.

ISBN 978-1-300-80945-6

Contents

1. The Present Crisis:
Imbalance between Economy and Culture

Today we are in the grip of a permanent "financial crisis" and a recession of the economy, which is regarded by those who study the matter seriously, as heralding the end of the present monetary system, and which, for this reason, has features that distinguish it from all previous crises. It is as if it had reached a low point from which it cannot rise towards a recovery through use of the methods that caused the débâcle. Yet this would appear to have been the intention behind the various state rescues of the bankrupted companies, and the aim of the EU in its desperation to prevent the financial collapse of its weaker members.

Such is the magnitude of the problem that, when one follows its development, it becomes clear that the present situation was not arrived at without someone being aware of what was happening. On the contrary, there was a deliberate movement towards the consequences of the collapse, the terminal crisis having been provoked by a financial élite raised above all states – a kind of super-state higher than all the states on the planet. At the present moment this élite is having to take steps towards the setting up of a world government and, therefore, gradually towards an organ that controls the issue of money, so that the various nations, including the United States, will be unable to regulate their economies because of interference in the issuing of their own money. These are gradual processes of centralization and gigantism of institutions, which separate them from their base and thereby make them more amenable to a centralized autocracy. Thanks to the enormous debt accumulated by the dollar, an attempt is being made to bring about a reform that will centralize the issue of money – and the country that presents the greatest obstacles to this is the United States itself. One may therefore guess that perhaps the moment has arrived to bring it to collapse – as the USSR was brought to collapse twenty years ago – in favour of a global centralization that is not disturbed in its plans by any kind of national interest.

The crisis, despite the difficulty it brings, is an opportunity to reflect upon and understand on a deeper level the meaning of the money and the finances of the world we live in, how we have reached historically the present situation and how we can work together to create a new monetary system. This is really necessary, in that the situation requires a movement for reform based on an understanding of the essential nature of money, and distancing itself – on the level of ideas to begin with – from the interests of the financial élite. It could be that the South American countries, particularly the group now referred to as ABC (Argentina, Brazil, Chile), are best equipped to take an initiative in this direction thanks to their ability to meet their own basic material needs. However, as a homogeneous critical mass has not been formed and our élites are susceptible to bribery, our systems are open to influence of any kind.

To compare the present crisis with the 1929 recession, the Great Depression in the inter-war period, in the latter case the usual statistic according to which only 10% of depositors reclaim their funds from the banks (enabling the remaining 90% to be used for loans) collapsed, as it became clear that the U.S.A. could no longer uphold the fiction that the dollar was still convertible into gold. Far more dollars had been issued than it was possible to provide a backing for, and the big financiers undertook an action to relieve themselves of the responsibility for the uncontrolled issue of dollars. They withdrew from the stock exchange and when, as a result of the shares' collapse on so-called "Black Thursday" (24th October), customers wished to reclaim their funds and the loans had to be transferred from the small to the large banks, the banking system crashed in favour of the big financiers of the Federal Reserve, who constituted for this event a cartel which was shortly to become a monopoly. In fact, it was from this moment that it became impossible for North American citizens to be reimbursed in gold, this right being restricted to States and banks throughout the world. Then as a further step, in 1933 during the Roosevelt presidency, there took place an incredible confiscation of all gold in citizens' possession and it was declared illegal to possess the metal, on the pretext that this would help the country out of the economic depression.

But the present financial crisis cannot be directly compared with that of 1929. If we follow step by step the gradual evolution of money and its backing, or the right to issue money, and at the same time the struggle implied in the parallel that exists between the evolution of money's significance and the evolution of human consciousness in the battle for a growing spiritual experience in freedom, we see that finance – which

6

is not the same as economy – and culture are in conflict with one another. If we inquire more deeply into their connection, the question arises: What is the most direct relation between the two? In the first place, and owing to the form in which, at present, power to issue dollars is granted to the Federal Reserve – the central bank of the U.S.A. (FED) – we have to do with a permanent authorization of a limitless expansion of the egoism of its holders, as the FED is a private corporation with a pseudo-public appearance. In chapter 4 we will list some of the events that have led to the present decline of the economic system and its absorption into the system of international finance.

Money, which also has to represent the value of the spiritual needs of man on the Earth, has been transforming itself exclusively into a representative of the needs of the body. It is an abstraction which expresses the value allotted to the various kinds of goods, a regulatory and non-substantial entity, and it is for this reason that its control by the forces of unbounded egoism of the financial élites strives to, and can, impede spiritual development.

Spiritual needs have to be assigned a value and financed, and in the past this has been done by states in the compulsory form of the payment of taxes for the financing of education and public health. But in the process of absorption of politics by the economy – and of this by finance – culture is forced more and more into a direction that suits those with the financial power. The retarding forces of evolution are fundamentally interested in gaining control of the issue of money, since they recognize that, through operating as a monopoly, they can control society and influence the ascent of human consciousness to a higher level; in other words, they can place the peoples of the world entirely into their service. But even so, in the last resort man's consciousness, which grows and individualizes itself, is an intangible that cannot be controlled by money. Despite the almost insuperable difficulty of progressing in this direction, the human being, who represents a "cosmic weight" in evolution, can be the intangible cause of events that are unforeseen by the retarding forces, who only understand the outer, material aspect of the world and not the spiritual morality inherent in human destiny. It is therefore important, if we are to awaken to the problems of our time, that we should understand the process of the relation between the present economic-financial crisis and the cultural-spiritual-ethical life of mankind.

The crisis of 1929 was one of the first big financial crises of the 20th century, which opened up for discussion the question of the meaning of money and the gold standard and demanded clarification of the relation of money to the production of consumer goods, the basic right to issue banknotes, and who had granted themselves this right. The consequences of this were that Congressman Louis McFadden, who lodged protests on these matters in the U.S. Congress, was the target of two assassination attempts and was finally poisoned. From then on, life in the 20th century accelerated continually, with the result that no-one could reflect upon and understand what was happening, still less draw up a balance of the monetary situation or of their own life. The Second World War came, and the debate regarding the authority and the fundamental right to issue money was entirely forgotten, much to the convenience of those who had granted themselves – we will see how – the power to issue it, i.e. primarily the U.S. Federal Reserve: *"Today the debate over who should create the national money supply is rarely heard, mainly because few people even realize it is an issue. Politicians and economists, along with everybody else, simply assume that money is created by the government, and that the "inflation" everybody complains about is caused by an out-of-control government running the dollar printing presses. The puppeteers working the money machine were more visible in the 1890s than they are today, largely because they had not yet succeeded in buying up the media and cornering public opinion."*[1]

The present financial crisis became evident in the U.S.A. with the so-called credit crisis of sub-prime mortgages during the year 2008 – that is, the problem of non-repayment of the credits granted to the huge number of mortgage bearers considered risky. At the time of the fall of the Twin Towers on 11th September 2001, the chairman of the Federal Reserve (a Corporation we will discuss later), who was at that moment, and had been for more than a decade, Alan Greenspan, lowered the interest gained by investors through the purchase of U.S. Treasury notes to a mere 1%, so that consumption would not fall in such a crisis period and the strength of the domestic economy of the U.S.A. could be maintained. The FED is a corporation parallel to the government, federal only in name as it has a virtually private character. It is the body responsible for fixing interest rates in the U.S.A. and issuing the amount of dollars it considers appropriate, and, since the dollar is the general reserve currency, the entire world is affected by this currency issue. The lowering of interest resulted in private investors refusing to continue investing in state bonds which up to that moment had been a

---

[1] Hodgson Brown, Hellen – The Web of Debt – Introduction: Money in the Land of Oz – Fifth Edition January 2012.

profitable investment, and, given the resulting cash surplus, international banks of all kinds were able to obtain cheap credit and sought opportunities to reinvest the borrowed money at a higher rate of interest than 1%. International credit funds had of necessity to find other channels of investment, and began increasingly to try to obtain higher gains from loans with insufficient security – or one should rather say the sale of their capital – going so far as to promote without limit the trade in mortgage purchases of an insecure or sub-prime character, in the certainty that if they were not repaid, the homes would be confiscated. In other words, they started to lend money to anyone who asked for it, thereby creating a bubble of growth in the price of properties due to the disproportionate demand resulting from the excess of credit. The world economy is continually growing – so people said – while money was being issued and loans were made. It was known, but no-one was troubled by the fact, that the excess of credit was lacking in the security of repayment on which credit is normally based, given that the conditions that had applied hitherto had been abandoned – namely, that one should lend only a percentage of the value of the property and that, in addition, the debt would be guaranteed by income and by other debtors. The thought was, simply, that if the money is not repaid the houses will be auctioned off, and the loan thus became a "present" for almost anyone, at the risk of the banks which, dazzled by the immediate gains, seemed only to see how their financial capital was growing. But, as was to be expected, the sub-prime customers were not able to repay their mortgages and began to default, one by one and en masse, causing the bubble of the bonanza of easy money to burst in the spring of 2008. Properties started to fall in price, creating a vicious circle and prompting more debtors to stop repaying their credits, as these were starting to be higher than the value of the properties and were no longer worth the trouble. Many houses with continually falling prices were auctioned off by the banks and, having been abandoned by the tenants, whole districts in some U.S. towns were given up to pillage, leading some to propose today that bulldozers should be brought in to flatten the area.

The matter is not so simple as we have described it here, since it involves a whole chain of investors of different types, and financial instruments known generically as derivatives – packets of credits and securities, all of which elements are difficult to understand exactly unless one is a specialist or devotes time to their study (sub-prime mortgages, packets of collateral obligatory debt, financial swaps of unpaid credits, etc.). The investors, eager to benefit from huge gains arising from the cheap loan of money in growing quantities, include institutions administering pension funds, mutual funds for investment on the stock exchange, security companies etc., mediated by the dealers on Wall Street – all of these, investors of different sorts seeking to increase their gains by way of the concept of "leverage". This acts like a lever, whereby the longer the arm, the less effort is required; and in financial terms it means to acquire on loan the largest amount possible in order to increase the benefits of an operation which, if carried out with little capital, does not realize as succulent gains as when the loan capital is extended with the help of cheap credit.

Quite apart from a specific understanding of the crisis that involves us all, it is worth looking at its purely quantitative aspect. Reference is often made to the process of abstraction which money has undergone in the course of evolution, from an economy based initially on barter, then to a monetary economy based on grain, archetypally wheat, then on gold, to arrive finally at the economy of today, based on credit. It is interesting to note the difference between the wheat standard, relating concretely to our need for food, and the credit standard, arising from the abstraction of money, which in reality is based on trust in human capacities. They are extremes of an even stronger polarity, which involves an understanding of the meaning of human life, because money, as a mirror of the evolution of the thought-process, exemplifies outwardly the necessary process of abstraction of man's mental life. If we wish to inquire into its significance, we have to ask what is its equivalent in the mental process. Here, one thing is the atom (which we cannot see) as the fundamental element of which the world consists, and its unconscious use in the practice of abstraction, and another is the development of the power of abstraction of pure thinking (without a basis as percept in sensory experience). With regard to money, it suffices to accept, to begin with, that we have on the one hand the abstraction of money through its virtual transformation into an enormous quantity and, on the other, the use of the machine for its movement with the quality that is consciously implanted in it.

The concept of money based on the credit standard is a difficult abstraction to grasp, and more difficult still to experience inwardly, because it implies that money at the present time is not a positive value, but a debt, requiring us to perform something like a crazy head-over-heels in our thinking, because normally money is ascribed a positive value, insofar as what the human being can offer society or needs to receive from it represents a value. Usually money is regarded solely as an expression of purely material needs and capacities, and the fact is ignored that, in the balance between needs and capacities – that is, between what is lacking and what can be offered – the human being also has spiritual needs and capacities. Money-as-debt means that the creditor counts what he is owed as an asset, he has taken illicit possession of what he has not yet been paid and, worse still, achieves by political means the issue of banknotes corresponding to his debt, taking possession of these and establishing a supposed right or credit, and lends it out again in an unlimited chain of loans which continue to fictitiously increase his capital. We will study later the meaning of the evolution of lending and its present distortion, the negative counterpart to a real evolutionary necessity which inclines towards the creation of a balance between human needs and capacities. Regarded as a whole, these two have an economic and a spiritual aspect.

The moneylender is reliant upon those people with the power to produce banknotes, which in theory has been granted to sovereign states for the purpose of administering labour and the collaboration between their inhabitants. However, this power, through the imposition of ever fewer conditions and the acceleration of processes thanks to computer technology, has surreptitiously shifted towards the private sector. The U.S.A. issues dollars which, imposed as control or reserve money, does not cause domestic inflation however great the quantity used. This does happen in other countries which, when they issue their own money in excess, generate a disproportionate money supply, causing a rise in prices in the market for goods and services. The right to issue money rests upon the responsibility and the capacity of states – the centre of balance between the market and civil society – to levy taxes which the citizens pay out of their labour; that this right has been usurped by private bodies is an act of robbery. The idea that has become prevalent is that, the more you can lend, including what you do not yet own but lend out all the same, the more debt-money you possess, and to this illicit money a value is assigned. I am owed money in the future, and not only do I count it up, but I lend it, whereby the debt acquires a positive character in the abstraction of the circulation of what does not yet exist, because money is being lent, to the power of one, two, three, etc. Each time, a more distant future is being mortgaged and the abstract money continues to grow thanks to the accrued interest, but its value is far from maintaining a connection with material or spiritual reality. Because this non-money represents a debt. Human spiritual capacities have been underrated, through the linking of money with finance in the first place and with the economy in the second. Ultimately, this situation expresses an absolutely unconscious confidence in the human spiritual capacities that are not valued, because the quantity of abstract money is so great, that it does not have a physical counterpart. Since the quantity of money in circulation is so incalculable, and so rapid its constant growth, the only possible way of translating it into reality is to regard it as a representative of human capacities – those which we know exist, but to which it is difficult to awaken; and they have been undervalued because they presuppose the overcoming of materialism, a stage that was necessary for the strengthening of the 'I'. What rules at the present time is "Money means not Money,"[2] in the words of the English economist Arthur Edwards. In this situation of the excess of money which generates an unhealthy credit there is an inversion towards the future – this is what credit always is – that is to say, there is a surplus that is wrongly directed, which needs to be understood in its evolutionary and not merely corrupt sense. Later on, we will try to help towards an understanding of it.

On the level of abstraction that we have reached today, money is not even an entry in a ledger; it is a virtual Excel number on the computer screen, which moves and changes at a vertiginous rate and does not allow us to know how much we are talking about, concretely; though this is of little importance, because it is too much. We need only mention the confusion arising in translations of all kinds of articles on economics, because what is called "one billion" in the Anglo-Saxon countries is not translatable as "un billón" in the Spanish-speaking world, although it is often translated thus out of ignorance, while at other times it is translated correctly, with immense confusion arising as a result. An Anglo-Saxon billion is equivalent to 10 raised to the 9th power, that is, a one with nine noughts, or one thousand million; while "un billón" is equivalent to 10 raised to the power of 12, that is, a one with twelve noughts, which is what the Anglo-Saxon call "a trillion" and not "un billón" as we do. This problem with number is a clear example of how quantity has risen so far into quantitative abstraction that this degree of alienation from reality shows that we need to understand the problem in a new, qualitative form, because we have got lost in numbers and don't know what we are talking about. For example, when we are told that, according to The Economist magazine, the global system exceeds two billion dollars of virtual transactions per day, in many cases we do not know for certain whether the translation has been done correctly, and which billion is meant. In other words, we mostly don't know how much we are dealing with. But what does it

---

[2] http://www.arthuredwards.net/

matter? – Because in either case it is a lot, and exceeds the ordinary person's power of comprehension.

It is clear that what has come to be called the real economy is one thing, and finance is another. The real economy expresses the relation of human needs to the resources that derive from the earth, while finance is the administering of money for money's sake, independently of concrete needs. This assumption is reflected in the fact that a number of leading newspapers, particularly in the northern hemisphere, have a financial supplement which does not form a part of the economic supplement, economy and finance being regarded as separate subjects. Of the daily movement quoted of 2 billion (with 12 noughts), the figure given by The Economist, 5% corresponds to the real economy and the remaining 95% is a financial game of "derivatives" and other speculative instruments. It is worth noting that what is known as the market in "derivative" speculative financial instruments did not exist in 1998; in 2002 it grew to 104 billion dollars, and in 2008 it grew to 531 billions (both figures with 12 noughts). The latter amount is equivalent to ten times the world's gross domestic product and forty times the GDP of the U.S.A. These figures show us the terminal nature of the present crisis, because unless we consider that there are in the world intangible spiritual values which are not accounted for in the balance, we do not know to what all this money refers or how many more bubbles are going to burst. There is a real counterpart – of which we will speak later – to the fact of the corruption in the realm of finance due to the failure to create the necessary flow of money from the economy for the financing of the development of intangible or spiritual values.

What we are experiencing at the present moment is, unquestionably, not an economic but a financial crisis. Despite unfairness in distribution, there would seem to be more than enough of commodities and the money that represents them; and the financial crisis speaks directly of a moral or ethical crisis, in a world in which the value of spiritual goods has been forgotten, and the surplus accumulates in the form of abstract money that has acquired the character of toxic assets – as they are quite openly referred to in the present crisis.

Despite its abuse in parasitic speculation, this does not imply a demonizing of the economy based on credit. The crisis should, rather, provide us with the opportunity to understand in depth the meaning of credit, the economic process and the significance of money, and trust that, given the effort of people of good will, there will come an understanding of the need for a movement of healthy monetary reform in each country of the global world.

One essential point to be understood and valued is – if you will pardon the tautology – the concept of value, which is not the same as price, but asks what value the human being attaches to the different things he needs for his existence. Value inclines, on the one hand, towards tangible goods or commodities and, on the other, towards the intangible goods that emerge on the level of culture (benefits of a scientific, aesthetic and moral nature arising from the spheres of science, art and religion). That is, on the one hand value is something that stems from the economic sector, in the first instance the archetype of agriculture, while on the other hand it is something that stems from the cultural sector. Agriculture and culture, two polar aspects of human social activity, form in the end a circle of necessary collaboration.

This has brought us to a particular aspect of economy: the financial crisis and its relation to the cultural crisis. We must look more deeply into the relation between these two factors, because this polarity between needs and capacities – physical and spiritual in each case – lives in the soul of the human being. On the path towards the satisfaction of both aspects, we can unfold a positive vision in contrast to what is one-sidedly termed the "financial crisis", which seems from the specific standpoint of the science of economics to be insoluble, because this science appears to be unable to think the interrelation of all the factors that influence the individual and human society. Now that the world has been globalized and has turned itself into a single and self-contained economic system (so long, at least, as we are not trading with extraterrestrials), many of the current economic theories do not apply, because they are built on the assumption of national economies, an outdated concept of open systems which can trade with one another in favour of the development of – in theory – each country. But as there are no longer nations, the Earth is, from the economic point of view, a global system and the states are enterprises... (with presidents equivalent to managers with power over a specific territory and authority with respect to the rights and obligations of its inhabitants). So long as our vision of society is not altered, the supra-national élites will be those who benefit.

We do not need to examine further the social phenomenon, as there is no question of a lack of money or productive capacity. What is affecting large masses of the world population is the tremendous injustice in social distribution. Full technological capacity and the

14

production needed were surpassed long ago, and there would be enough for everyone if there were a fair distribution. To bring just one example of the depth of the human cultural crisis we need only cite the widespread psychological problems arising in situations of material abundance, the absence of values on the level of spirituality and human feeling, the high rates of suicide and violence among large numbers of young people who are not without money or credit cards for spending on consumer goods – just to mention one sector of the population of the big cities in East and West.

Let us see how, in practice and in the ideals of human society, this polarity of economy and culture comes to expression, which, archetypally, can also be described as: agriculture and culture, earth and heaven, body and spirit.

2. The Threefold Structuring of Society and its Ideals: Civil Society, State and Market – Liberty, Equality and Fraternity

Three differentiated sectors of human activity constitute society in its archetypal form: the political, economic and cultural sectors, or in socio-political terms: the state, the market and civil society in their independent activity. Finance does not belong to the economy in the strict sense, but is a distortion in the management of money, causing it to lose its connection with real values.

Every human activity is embraced within one of these sectors and, although they interpenetrate in their mutual influences and relations, each one has its own specific characteristics and ideals. It would be appropriate for them to have each an independent administration, an independence that would not exclude mutual collaboration – that is, they will become interdependent. It can be asserted that the ideals of the three sectors were first formulated during the French Revolution, since liberty, equality and fraternity are the ideals, respectively, of culture, the political life and economy. In 1789 they appeared in history with premature vehemence in the first awakening of the bourgeoisie to democracy, and it was not possible to advance further than their mere proclamation owing to the immaturity of human consciousness. In post-revolutionary France, the immediate corruption began, of the supposedly newborn social system. The ideals appeared in the realm of thought, but could not be referred or assigned to the three differentiated social sectors. For Rudolf Steiner: "The totality of the social organism will form as a result of the independent separating-out of each of these three spheres."[3]

The threefold structuring of society in the sectors we have mentioned – culture, political life and economy, or civil society, state and market – is linked to the relation established by the human being to three decisive aspects of his individual life. When in search of life's

---

[3] Steiner, Rudolf – Spiritual Science and the Social Question.

meaning, the human being relates to himself on an intimate level, there arise out of his own inner activity questions that lead him to what others have thought on this or that subject in the course of history and, better equipped, he can then think about the world and form his own convictions in all areas of the cultural life: religious or moral, aesthetic and scientific. This aspect of individual human activity and its expression needs to be realized in complete freedom, of both consciousness and outer expression. Two questions are enough to enable us to grasp the essence of the ideal of freedom in the cultural sector: How can something we wish for spiritually be attained, if not through absolute freedom of thought? How can the objects of cultural striving be valued in a society in which the attempt is made to condition the power of comprehension and evaluation in the larger part of the population through State policies on education and health? Freedom is the ideal precondition for the development of a healthy cultural life.

Secondly, when the human being relates to the physical world, the material substance which is given to us by the earth for our subsistence and is for us a basic need, he brings about the economic life, by means of which – through the working together of human beings – the needs of the body are satisfied. Today's economy is based on the postulate of the scarcity of resources and, therefore, of the need for population control so that the earth's resources might not prove insufficient. The extreme sectors of the government élites also use this justification for population control, for which the most sinister methods are applied (something that was already proposed in the 18th century by the English economist Thomas Malthus[4]). All the eugenic projects that have been initiated in the world rest on the foundation of Malthusianism. An example of this is a monument in the U.S. state of Georgia – known as the Georgia Guidestones[5], which is regarded as America's Stonehenge – with various commandments for a post-Apocalyptic society, which

---

[4] Malthusianism is an economic theory put forward by the British economist Thomas Malthus (1766-1834), according to which the rate of population growth follows a geometric progression, while the rate of increase of resources needed for its survival follows an arithmetical progression. This means that if factors such as famine, war, plague, etc., did not reduce population numbers, the birth of children who are insufficiently provided for would gradually impoverish the human race and even lead to its extinction. This contrasts with the theory of those who believed in the unlimited perfectibility of the human race.

[5] The Georgian Guidestones are a monument of five large stones near Eberton, Georgia, U.S.A., built mysteriously in 1979, and engraved with a Decalogue in several ancient and modern languages, giving advice on how to live on the Earth, in a post-Apocalyptic scenario.

include the intention to practise population control. But a mentally sound human being 'knows' that all of us on the earth have a right to live here, and that the organization of society must be possible, since it is not a question of lack of natural resources, but of injustice in distribution. Without doubt, the ideal of the economic life is fraternity, that is, the sharing of resources and developing of human capacities so that what is produced extends to all of earth's inhabitants. The control of population can only arise from the will of the individual based upon a free moral comprehension of the problem.

And finally, when human beings enter into relation with one another for the organization of life in common, taking account of rights and obligations for the administration of public life, there emerges the political life of the nation-state in which they were born and/or live. And this is where problems arise, because the social life implies that one person enters into relation with another, regardless of the different needs and capacities of each one. Simply through the fact that we are human beings, we have the same rights. Equality is the ideal of the political life.

The threefold structuring of human social life – and the requirement of independence for each of the three sectors – is not an arbitrary, theoretical division worked out intellectually and then applied to society like an economic methodology or state planning policy. It depends upon the free activity of the individual human beings who initiate it. As Steiner shows, this independence of the three social sectors has its root in the constitution of the individual human being, which is also a threefold organism in its bodily, soul and spiritual aspect. The relation that exists between the evolution of the individual human being – his faculties and also his physical constitution – and the social system, is a very close one, and it is the individual who must develop the capacity to realize within himself that which allows him to advance towards a society with these characteristics. Consider, for example, how a social organism is influenced by an individual who has succeeded in overcoming the indiscriminate mixing of emotions (linked up to his own life and personal interests) with the thoughts that are seeking to arrive at the truth. If a social balance is to be found and the present crisis overcome through a drastic reduction of the toxic instruments that are destroying society, we as individuals must – in increasing numbers and in free associations – bring about within ourselves changes that can manifest initially in the organizing of small groups and institutions, which will radiate the virtues of this independence and the will of the three sectors to work in collaboration with one another. That is to say, each one of us needs to understand the correspondence that exists between individual and society. If we remove the toxic elements that live in the individual soul – which are the ultimate causes of the toxicity in society – we will bring cleansing to the social milieu in which we live. We cannot think of change unless we succeed in creating an environment in which individual transformation is gently encouraged. Marxism is a clear example of the way an idea has first to be thought in order, then, to be put into practice, and in this sense one needs to be able to think the relation between the constitution of the human being and the social system[6], and the transformation of both in the course of evolution. The parallelism and the interdependency implied in it form a part of the proposal to relate the individual's path of knowledge to the social system.

The path towards this transformation is based on trust in the virtue of the human being who, simply through the fact of being human, is able, when he grasps something with a healthy intellect, to inwardize it and involve his feelings, and then try to act accordingly. Though what we are putting forward here may sound naïve, it is the only possible way for humanity to evolve. It is not a matter of doing for the sake of doing, but of action on the basis of thought; what society is suffering from is not a lack of ability to launch materialistic enterprises. Evolution as a whole is not abstract and cannot be based on anything other than the evolution of individuals. Undoubtedly, in more backward countries individual development is made extremely difficult, as transformation begins on the cultural level (in the South American countries, for example, which in the course of several centuries of authoritarianism have been laid waste culturally). But it is important to remark that we live in an epoch of individual development and the social milieu has an influence, but not a decisive one.

Belief in the virtue inherent in the human being does not mean that we stop seeing, or that we naively accept, the fact that there are sectors of society which do not wish to understand the social problem and have no interest whatever in resolving it, because they know full well that this could go against their interests and because they are also consciously motivated by the forces of uncontrolled egoism and corruption. Moreover, parallel to the development of the political systems towards democracy, groups have been forming, with a deliberate orientation towards the domination of the consciousness of other human beings, on both the psychic and physical level. With the

---

[6] Steiner, Rudolf – Spiritual Science and the Social Question.

aim of using them as instruments for the attainment of their own goals, they have spared no effort through the medium of education, medicine and nutrition. The age of obvious physical slavery is past, but not the impulse behind it, as the methods used for the purpose of domination are now far more subtle. Since the awakening that has taken place into the nature of the economic process, the problems of the social organism can no longer be solved through the subjugation of a part of the population, even if the methods are now more subtle. By means of the domination of consciousnesses, human beings can be deceived and the will of such élite groups can be put into effect concealed behind clever political manoeuvres, or through the – expediently occult – instilling of fear, or else directly by means of war, hunger and other extreme measures, in places where the unbridled struggle for power and natural resources is more evident.

World domination has been, explicitly, a goal throughout western history – essentially from the time of the extinction of the earlier, innate powers of clairvoyance, when it became absolutely necessary to organize society according to different criteria in ancient Rome. At the present time, after the bloodshed of the 20th century, nothing could lead one to think that the Anglo-Saxon élites, the victors of the world wars, had learned anything of the possibility of a harmonious coexistence of the nations – a concept which, on the other hand, also needs to be superseded because, in the last resort, it leads to nationalism. It is hardly surprising that in these first moments of a global experience of the unity of the Earth – and of an understanding of the way the Earth belongs spiritually to the universe – a struggle of this kind should have been unleashed for the power to set up a global government. The abstract nature of money and its infinite multiplication are a reflection of the potency that has been attained by the human spirit, manifesting in the capacity of invention and production on an Earth which, viewed within a higher geometrical dimension, is infinite, and which we are persuaded to look upon as limited and possessing scant resources.

The Earth viewed as an entity belonging to the universe undoubtedly has infinite resources, since to regard it as a limited or finite entity is a short-sighted scientific perspective. After all, it is the sun which transforms the inert matter of the Earth into living substance in the plant world – a miracle if we can observe it out of a full grasp of the difference between the dust of the Earth and the transformed substance in the body and the form of the plant kingdom.

21

From the perspective of modern science, specifically from that of projective geometry – which is the most conceptual of the non-Euclidian or post-Einsteinian geometries – we know that the Earth is, effectively, an infinite entity. This concept does not contradict an understanding of the finite as set down in Euclidian geometry, but, as we can grasp it in pure thought, it implies an experience of the finite world as an aspect of a far more complex cosmos. Projective geometry speaks of a substantial infinite very different from the abstract infinite of experimental science, which one tries to reach with the help of satellites and other contrivances. To grasp the concept of geometrical infinity can set us on the path towards a higher consciousness. When we have reached our own limit, in the observation of how we make ourselves conscious we advance a few steps in this direction. Man is a spiritual being capable of an ardent enthusiasm for the truth and the determination to realize it in practice. Confrontation, sacrifice and pain are in any case an unavoidable part of evolution and of training in the ability to develop the real human capacities. Changes that are qualitatively significant, though quantitatively small, can have an influence on the destiny of humanity. We are living at a time where there is an increasing division taking place between those who, in the core of their being, have a yearning for the good – which does not imply a negation of evil, but its overcoming – and those who consciously involve themselves in evil for the sake of their own advantage. This does not mean they must be dismissed out of hand, or excluded altogether from the idea of redeemable humanity, but the conscious involvement with evil – and not with error, which it is human to fall into – is a deep question which exceeds the limits of the present work. In his book 'Leviathan', Hobbes already spoke of a division of humanity into those who struggle for the good and those who compromise with evil; this can only raise the question as to the redemption of evil.

The ideas concerning the threefold constitution of the human being – as an entity consisting of physical body, soul and spirit (and the last two differentiated within themselves) – are a fundamental contribution of the Austrian philosopher Rudolf Steiner (1861-1925), who laid the foundations for an understanding of the physiological, soul and spiritual threefoldness of the human being. The 'I' of man, his absolutely individual being, lives in the central core of his soul and is an eternal entity which can take upon itself responsibly the causes and consequences of its own life. The soul is the entity that mediates with the earth and is the place where live the tensions that arise between bodily and spiritual needs, for the sake of the evolution of the individual 'I'. After having developed these concepts in depth in the transition from the 19th to the 20th century in the discipline which he called spiritual science or Anthroposophy, Steiner also put forward ideas for the constitution of what he referred to as a new social order. "(…) in 1905, just at the moment when the alliances for the First War were being ratified, he presented the outline of a new social form in the magazine 'Lucifer Gnosis' (translated as 'Spiritual Science and the Social Question'), where he brought forward the first elements for harmonization of the conflict between Nation and State." His proposals, of crucial significance, included the need to take steps to avoid the catastrophe that was looming at the beginning of the 20th century, in that the contrast between communism and capitalism was already appearing. We should point out that a new social order is not the same as a new world order.

The year 1905 was important in the history of the 20th century, because behind the scenes the secret alliances were being formed, which would lead to the First War, with the aim of protecting the interests of the Anglo-Saxon élites, who were already making advances in the corrupt use, to their own advantage, of the media of communication. These élites were beginning to feel threatened by the centre of Europe, particularly the German state of Prussia which had been formed through a process of military expansion – a betrayal of the Romantic ideals of expansion by way of cultural influence. The Prussian state was potentially a dangerous union of forces of Central Europe with Russia (in the formation of the dreaded Eurasia), which would impede the global commercial supremacy striven for by the British Empire, associated from the beginning with private business élites in the advance of liberalism. After the First World War, with the defeat of Germany and the Austro-Hungarian Empire, that is, the first destruction of Middle Europe and its possible harmonizing rôle between East and West, first steps were taken towards the formation of an East-West bipolarity: on the one hand the Russian Marxist-Leninist revolution of 1917 which gave rise to the communist bloc and, on the other, the transfer of commercial and financial hegemony from London to New York. It was the beginning of the antithesis between communism and capitalism, which finally unfolded during the Cold War after the total destruction of middle Europe – and, actually, also of Russia – at the conclusion of the Second World War.

It was after the First War that Steiner viewed it as absolutely necessary that the centre of Europe, Germany in particular, should come forward

– in contrast to the western world which had defeated it – with ideas that would allow the ground to be laid for a new social structure. He saw the need for the creation, in each State, of a cultural sector independent of the political bodies and of the economic market, cultural sectors that would be able – essentially in the schools – to bring citizens together as individuals outside the framework of the multiple nationalities imposed politically. These would radiate spiritual forces, and thereby make possible the formation of states of a basically cultural character, independent of the arbitrary distinctions resulting from the political fixing of borders. The need to overcome nationalisms and seek relations between human beings as individuals – this was his underlying idea already then. As he said, this was the only possible way towards a peaceful constitution of the states of Central Europe, thereby averting another war on multi-ethnic lines and across many artificial borders, which is what would actually come about after the 1919 Treaty of Versailles. This was the geopolitical configuration that was encouraged by the Fourteen Points of the North American President Woodrow Wilson, proposing a so-called "self-determination" of the peoples, but which in reality came about under the custodianship of emerging international institutions which would recognize the incipient claim of the U.S.A. to assume the role of international vigilante. For the central European states it is in fact impossible – concretely and through destiny – to defend their borders by political-military means, and instead of war, the antiquated way of constituting themselves as nations, they should engage with new ideas regarding the formation of free multicultural states.

The ideas of the new social order proposed by Steiner will be the lens through which, in this work, we will view the symptomatology of the financial crisis, seeking to contribute elements that may show how a solution can be found. As we mentioned earlier, there is a connection between the inner path of individuals and the possibility of realizing these ideas on the social level. The idea of the administrative, functional separation within human society, of the three sectors of which it consists, corresponds to the path of the individual human being and the attainment of a certain, increasing, level of independence of his three soul faculties – his life of thought, his life of soul or feeling and the life of his will-impulses. To be able to come to an understanding with others on the level of spiritual objectivity, the human being must confront his own sympathies and antipathies more and more consciously. In the life of ordinary consciousness these three faculties are intermixed and the human being cannot confront feelings and will-

24

impulses, which are peculiar to each individual, in an objective way – that is, as if they were objects of the world which appear in consciousness in the manner of something external to the core of the 'I'. Only through conscious effort in the core of the 'I', which is where the basis lies for individual evolution, can the world be experienced in universal form and not merely oriented towards one's own subjective interests. The human being must be able, gradually, to confront what he feels and the impulses of his own particular will, with the growing forces of a thinking trained in an understanding of the universal significance of human life on the Earth and in the universe. Only when self-education of this kind is made inward, does the human being acquire the capacity to be morally objective towards himself – that is, to see himself as objectively as though he were another, a third person. This inner path would eventually lead towards the independence of the three social sectors, thus enabling them to make the right decisions in the spheres for which they are responsible.

The parallelism between the three sectors of society and the threefold structure of the individual human being, both in his body and physiological systems, and in his soul faculties – thinking, feeling and willing – and in the states of consciousness of his spiritual life (conscious in his life of thought, semi-conscious in his life of feeling, and unconscious in his will impulses – or, in Steiner's terminology, waking consciousness, dreaming consciousness and sleeping consciousness), can be studied more deeply and from many points of view as a theme of spiritual science.

For its proper functioning, the cultural sector needs money to flow to it from the economic sector, and this happens via the State on a compulsory basis through the payment of taxes – a 'forced donation' made by the economic sector to the cultural sector. Humanity will need to evolve much further before it makes the donation voluntarily, at which time, through a reconsideration of the concept of taxation and redistribution of money, a path of progress in this area will be able to emerge – a theme we cannot deal with further in the present work. There is enough space to add that this redistribution of money does not, on any account, imply the right of the State to interfere in the concerns of the cultural sector. We can see how this works on a primitive level as we observe life in a small village: its inhabitants bartered among themselves the produce cultivated and the manufactured articles; but the spiritual workers, for example, the priest and the schoolmaster, received these commodities from other people because their work did not produce what was needed for the subsistence of the body; their work was and had to be valued by their fellow-men in order for them to be able to continue to provide this service. At the present time, thanks to technological development and the saving of time and energy, we have been moving into a social reality in which there are more and more people who are able to cultivate their spiritual capacities, in order to place them in the service of society.

3. A Brief History of the Development of Social Organization – and: Why is it Difficult for a Free and Independent Cultural Sector to Emerge?

From one point of view – in the final chapter we will discuss the question from a different point of view – thinking is the soul faculty which was the last to develop in the evolution of humanity. And although this came about in Greece, it was still imbued with a certain spontaneous perception of the next higher world to the physical, which Aristotle called the world of the quintessence or the ethereal world – a world lying beyond the four elements which form life on the Earth. Proof of the late emergence of thought unmixed with the other qualities of man's inner life – that is, as a product of man's will and not as something merely perceived or as a gift intermixed with spiritual elements – is the immensely powerful influence of Greek thought, which lasted more than fifteen centuries. Medieval Europe simply thought and rethought Platonism and Aristotelianism alternately until the Renaissance was well under way, and only in the 1500's did his maturity reach a point where the human being could liberate his intellectual forces and begin a scientific investigation of the physical world. He recognized that the physical world was the only one he could really perceive, and that he would have to reach through to spiritual content by other means. The forging of a human thinking capacity detached from spontaneous perception of the spiritual world was a long process that was becoming established little by little in the practice of thought itself. This process began during the revision of Aristotle by medieval Scholasticism, and only unfolded fully with Descartes in the 1600's in the post-Platonic or Aristotelian ideas and the birth of the first idealism.

The character of thought-activity, but not only in one direction, that is, thinking about what is external – micro or macroscopically, as in today's science – was the critical point at issue in the Renaissance debate between the alchemists of the 15th, 16th and 17th centuries and dogmatic Catholicism, which launched the subsequent persecutions.

However, it is difficult to understand correctly this parting of the ways, because the outward-oriented science was not so one-sided as that of the present day, in that it represented in itself a revolutionary step forward, through the fact that the process had just begun, of the freeing of human intellectual development from the dogmatically received revelation upheld by the Catholic Church. External science, very one-sided today, was at that moment an avant-garde, coherent mental process, working with bare sense-perception, which was only beginning to grasp the physical world in experience.

The intensification of such an activity of thought by means of a purely inner force, to the point where a new philosophy could build a bridge to spiritual perception, was still something very new and embryonic in humanity. After a long period of preparation it came to an intensive unfolding, for the first time, among the philosophers of the German Romantic movement in the 18th century. To provide a rational basis for the capacity of pure thinking was viewed by Rudolf Steiner, in his 'Theory of Knowledge of the Goethean World Conception' and his later 'Philosophy of Freedom', as a necessity for human evolution on the Earth, and was the central point of his philosophical work. Many leading scientists are now beginning to recognize the error of seeking exclusively in one direction and in external proof. A large number of them, faced with the difficulty of finding the invariability of matter in itself, also seek a connection with Buddhism and other Oriental philosophies. The activity of thinking in the immediate present has, on the level of practical philosophy, not yet been strengthened in itself, and this is why the consciousness of the average human being, which is still being moulded almost exclusively from outside – particularly, but not only, in the Latin countries – can be influenced and dominated by way of human emotions and feelings, especially and unquestionably through fear.

This is all well known to those who imposed the restriction on individual liberties at the time of the 11th September. They know that fear is an emotion that is closely linked to the path of individual freedom, since there is no freedom without the possibility of failure, which frightens us; but it is one thing to raise fear to consciousness in order to confront it, and quite another to have fear instilled into us by hidden means. It is individual weakness of this kind that explains why on the social level it has not yet been possible to forge a cultural pole independent of politics and economy. Obedience is elicited in exchange for bread, as Ivan says in his debate with Alyosha in 'The Brothers Karamazov'. Formation of the cultural pole requires the creation of an environment that fosters the ability to cultivate thought as a real experience, and this environment is not just difficult to create, but is easily thwarted by fear of the non-satisfaction of basic needs. It is not possible to elaborate on this here, but the history, and the necessity, of the various attempts and failures to create this independent cultural pole can be followed with the help of a thorough study.

Before the time of Christ, when spiritual or clairvoyant perception was a spontaneous gift in a world in which the human being was less individualized, the three social sectors worked in harmony under the spiritual guidance of the initiate – the Pharaoh, for example. Thus Hermes, the great Egyptian initiate, was regarded as king, lawgiver and priest, that is to say, he embraced fully the economic, political and spiritual functions, and because of the spiritual integrity of his Being, they were recognized by his contemporaries. In the individual human being the soul faculties were not yet individualized – a necessary condition for the supersensible perception experienced quite naturally in antiquity. The human being is individualized and separates himself from the universe when the thinking faculty is born, whereby a differentiated experience of outer and inner is established, obliging him to form from out of himself the motives that guide his action.

But after Christ who, from a non-dogmatic point of view, is the archetype of the incarnation of the free human 'I', the human being lost the spiritual perception which had been given to him by nature in the previous civilizations. The challenge he has to face is the beginning of a long path of individualization in which he can regain these capacities through his own effort. The view put forward here, which does not set limits to human thought, merits philosophical justification, but this will not be offered in the present work[7]. We will, however, make it clear that it is opposed to the Kantian conception, which prevails in the scientific mainstream and in the common consciousness of society today. In the conventionally held world-view the scope of human thinking has a limit which restricts it to the physical world and to mathematical abstraction, the spiritual factor being relegated to the sphere of religion and not of science, owing to its subjective character which sets it outside the realm of empirical objects.

As a result of the loss of connection with the higher world – which was the beginning of the incapacity of human beings to recognize each other's abilities – from Roman times onwards many of those who still

---

[7] Steiner, Rudolf – Philosophy of Freedom.

retained spiritual faculties came under the influence of corrupt forces and the organization of political life in a new way was understood to mean the creation of conditions of equity which would allow the full unfolding of the social life.

The three aspects of social life – economy, politics and culture – began to separate out after the coming of Christ, a parallel process to the separation of the human soul faculties (will, feeling and thinking). Both these processes – in the individual and in society – move towards the independence of their component parts, which will make possible a reunification through a matured consciousness. These processes of separation in the human soul can be studied historically on the level of the evolution of ideas.

Just when this evolutionary process begins, there emerges also its retrograde counterpart activated by the forces of opposition to evolution. The forces that fall behind in evolution always try to hold back the evolutionary impulses and, through doing so by means of capacities that have matured in the past, they succeed in exerting much influence, causing a retardation of the processes needed for the maturing of the new capacities, because they are afraid of losing power.

From the very beginning of the Christian epoch politics engulfs the cultural-spiritual life. We see the clearest example of this in the formation of the Catholic Church in the middle of the first three centuries of persecution in the Catacombs in the West and of the many relations existing between the nascent Christianity and the Gnostic streams in the Middle and Far East. Once the capital of the Roman Empire was transferred from Rome to Constantinople in the 4th century, the Church and its power remained without protection in Rome. Faced with the advance of the so-called "barbarian" peoples, which was fully justified from an evolutionary point of view, the Church assumed a political role, which strove for the predominance of Rome through the whole of Christendom. It is a well-known fact that it constituted itself, and not by chance, according to the authoritarian pyramidal forms of the decadent Roman Empire. From the time of its constitution, which is generally understood to have taken place at the Nicene Council of 324 A.D., its role as a victim of persecution during the Christianity of the Catacombs transformed itself – particularly after its institutionalization in 380 as the official religion of the Empire – into that of persecutor of the so-called heresies, and promulgator of the succession of anathemas and excommunications – i.e. persecutor of the free spiritual life.

The possibility of a free spiritual life was then embraced by the esoteric movements which started to operate clandestinely, not merely because of the need to cultivate spiritual knowledge in secret – as was the case with the Pythagorean school – but because of the persecutions which began with the establishment of the Church (directed first against the Manicheans, Arianism, Pelagianism, etc. and later against the Cathars and the Templars, to name only the most important movements). The persecutions continued and intensified until after the Renaissance, with the extermination of the Rosicrucians when the Counter-Reformation was launched under the leadership of the Jesuits as the militant branch of the Church, from the 16th and 17th centuries onwards[8].

Manichaeism, led by Manes in the 3rd century A.D., was a movement that sought to bring the new Christianity into harmony with the spiritual movements of the Far East – Persian Buddhism, Hinduism, and also the ancient Chinese wisdom – after having suffered persecution on account of the difference that emerged in its ranks with the theological position of Augustine of Hippo, known in the Church as Saint Augustine, one of the Fathers of the patristics of the Catholic Church. Arianism, a teleological view which sought to emphasize the substantial quality of the Son in the cosmic Trinity – closer to man than is the figure of God the Father – was excommunicated, but its influence continued for a long time in various parts of Europe.

The coronation of Charlemagne at the beginning of the 9th century is an important milestone in the subjugation of the cultural by the political life. At the time of Charlemagne the Catholic Church was struggling to assume the political role, and he as Emperor had resolved to separate the political from the religious sphere and thereby favour the development of an independent cultural life throughout his realm. How are we, then, to understand the transfer of political power into the hands of the Church? In Charlemagne's court there were two streams, a Latin and a Germanic, opposed to one another on the question of submission to Rome[9], while he sought to make himself independent of the Church. Of course, in the official history – supported in general by opinion of plainly Jesuit character – there is little mention of the German stream, which is deeply connected with the stream of King Arthur of the British Isles and with esoteric Christianity. In this silence it is not easy to hear something that is objectively known, since it is told even by Einhardt, Charlemagne's official biographer. We are referring to the disgust felt

---

[8] Yates, Frances – The Rosicrucian Enlightenment – 1972.
[9] Stein, Walter Johannes – The Ninth Century and the Holy Grail.

by Charlemagne when the Pope crowned him almost by surprise during his visit to Rome, as he had not gone for this reason, nor was he expecting it. In assuming the power to crown, the Pope was laying claim to a hierarchical superiority to which Charlemagne would not have wished to submit. His impulse was to establish a connection with the Catholic Church that would not imply a superiority of the Papal-religious power. The Emperor longed for freedom in the realm of culture and the political life, and had to distance himself from dogma, on its path to the infallibility of the Pope which had already been won by Rome. But on this point he failed and the Church imposed its authority.

As the centuries passed, some time after the Middle Ages the force of economy started to try to dominate political life, something that, with the onset of the Industrial Revolution and the emergence of the British Empire in the 18th century, began to develop to the full and has not stopped, even today.

Long before, in the 14th century, the Knights Templar saw the need to create an economic pole that was not only mercantile, but a pole from which the economy would work in harmony with spiritual development – that is, on the basis of its ideal of fraternity. They would see the need to attain this maturity just before the 'discovery of America', which was not a discovery but the opening up of a route already known to the Irish monks[10], and also to the Chinese and the Vikings. The Templars sought to take care of the gold and to develop a banking system of fraternal exchange so as to bring about a learning process and lay the cultural foundations that would prevent the plunder of gold when the time would inevitably come, for the discovery of America on a commercial level. Concealment of its existence up to that moment had been encouraged by certain Scottish and Irish religious orders, who wanted to protect it from private interests and to attain the maturity necessary for a worthy colonization. However, the Templars were destroyed in 1314 by the alliance of the French King Philippe Le Bel with Pope Clement V, who had been instated by the same French monarch. At the beginning of our scientific epoch, during the Renaissance when, in the reign of the Catholic kings and under the patronage of the Papacy of Alexander VI (patriarch of the Borgia family), the explorers reached America, there was now no way of preventing gold fever, and America was plundered.

---

[10] Steiner, Rudolf – Geographic Medicine – 17th November 1917 – St. Gallen, Switzerland.

A short time before, in the South of France, the Cathar movement had come into being. There is much debate as to whether they were on friendly terms or not with the Templars, in view of the fact that they did not belong to the Catholic Church or recognize its authority, unlike the Knights Templar, who only recognized the Papal authority, without the latter interfering in their hierarchical or internal decisions. In fact, their adherence or not to the Church was a factor that placed the Orders in real opposition to each other; nevertheless, there is conclusive evidence that many Cathars were protected by the Templars when their extermination began in the 13th century, and it is only thanks to this collaboration that one can explain the strength of their resistance until 1244. Together with the troubadour movement in Langued'oc and Langued'oil, which was avant-garde in that period, the Cathars developed a powerful independent cultural pole. They were feminists, vegetarians and pacifists – principles that were very advanced for their time and not tolerated by the political forces of the day, who exterminated them without trial. Not long afterwards the Templars were to be first tried and then exterminated.

Another crucial event that had a negative effect on the emergence of a cultural pole independent of political and economic forces was the Thirty Years War (1618-1648) in Middle Europe, between the princes of the Reformation lands in Germany and Bohemia and Catholicism supported by the Hapsburgs of Germany and Spain. Official history does not show that after so bloody a conflict any great changes had occurred (apart from the death of around 66% of the population of central Europe), as the Protestants and Catholics apparently carried on as before. But what is generally not mentioned, is the destruction of the Rosicrucian movement which, together with the alchemists and taking advantage of the new development of the printing-press, had initiated a significant cultural movement[11]. Around the court of Frederick of the Palatinate and his wife Isabel, daughter of the English King James I, they constituted a nascent cultural centre which Rome and the Hapsburgs viewed with displeasure. A major consideration was the fact that the cultural movement had, during the reign of Rudolf – a black sheep of the Hapsburgs who proved unsympathetic to the kind of interests pursued by them on the Continent – spread towards Prague[12]. The founding of the Jesuit Order and the Council of Trent, which lasted

---

[11] Yates, Frances – The Rosicrucian Enlightenment (1972) – Ideas and Ideals in the North European Renaissance (1984) – The Occult Philosophy in the Elizabethan Age (1979).
[12] ibid.

18 years, gave form to the persecution and espionage which began to confront the forces allied to Rome[13]. They would soon initiate an alternative strategy of repeated confrontations, but they would also form an alliance with new Anglo-Saxon elements that were awaiting their entrance into evolution, and also with the Masons, a movement which, while it should not be judged too one-sidedly, acted in the official sphere of English life as the emissaries of its industrial élite.

The French Revolution, as a political-cultural impulse, sought to free the political administration of the State from the confused intermingling of State and Church. As a result of the social struggle the separation of the two institutions came about, with the activity of the Church beginning to restrict itself to religion, but it was not possible to remove it from the cultural life. Although the ideals of liberty, equality and fraternity for human social life were born, the ability to understand them fully and to assign them their place within the context of the threefold structure of society, had not yet matured. They were applied wrongly to the different spheres and, adding to this the intrigues of the English élite pursuing their own interests, there flowed the deep corruption of the years of terror and the unfolding of the Napoleonic empire.

At the beginning of the 19th century, there were hints of a possible alliance of Napoleon with the forces of south-west Germany, the region that is now the state of Baden-Württemberg, thanks to the marriage of his adoptive daughter Stephanie with the Crown Prince Karl of Baden. This part of Germany, independent of Prussia and not Catholic, unlike Bavaria, was the cradle of Romanticism. It was here that the child of this couple was born, the heir to the Prince's throne, who would fulfil the conditions to bring about the harmony between the forces of political France and cultural Germany in the middle of Europe. But in the year 1833 the Kaspar Hauser affair occurred. It is assumed that he was assassinated by an emissary of the English lodges, who had no wish to see emerge in Middle Europe a force that could weaken its own influence. With the Kaspar Hauser assassination in 1833, a murder committed in accordance with spiritual principles which sought to destroy his 'I'-being and not just his physical body, a moment in the life of humanity begins, in which assassination comes to be an instrument of the secret societies and of espionage. This fact was discussed by Rudolf Steiner in a number of lectures, and in Germany today revelation of the true facts is still being sought. The age-old

---

[13] ibid.

esoteric societies begin to interfere in political-economic interests and it is hard to separate the wheat from the chaff.

In the first half of the 20th century one can already surmise that military conflict will give rise to the economic conflict of the second half, and at the present time a complete engulfment of the political sector by the economic is taking place. The outcome of the two World Wars was the destruction of Middle Europe, and the signal for the advance of the business and financial élites of Anglo-Saxon origin, who would shift to North America. There is an alliance with the Zionist forces – these are distinct from religious Judaism and do not coincide with the present State of Israel – which has been in effect for nearly three generations and which does not necessarily have to do with the original setting up of a military base in the Middle East allied to the U.S.A.

The outcome of the Cold War and its abrupt conclusion in 1989 was the downfall of the Russian people and the entry of the countries of Eastern Europe into the capitalist system. The trans-national élites who had financed the communist experiment – out of the ineluctable social need to confine it to one region – dropped the experiment suddenly, and Russia moved across from the one system to the other. The same communist nomenclatures were transformed overnight into successful bidders for the capitalist system, and were those who took it upon themselves to accept the influx of the dollar, which would pitilessly destroy Russian society which, after 70 years of communism had, without mediation or transition, to absorb the business way of life of capitalism. This destruction was assiduously described by Alexander Solzhenitsyn in his last books. It was as if, among the various methods of control used by the two hostile powers – communism and capitalism – the transnational financial élites intuited that the Western system of control with a television in every household would work much better than the system of control used by the communists, with a policeman on every street corner.

Starting with the apogee of Anglo-Saxon imperialism, the economy continued to overtake politics and culture in such a way that today we cannot even claim that democracy exists. What we have is an electoral political system in which the parties no longer represent any ideology, but are best described with the term "catch-all-party", taking it in turns, at most, to appear to function as a two-party system, but responding in reality to the financial incentives and lobbying of the big economic corporations, which are far more powerful.

Today the main dynamic lies on the level of finance and not of the real economy, because in the course of the 20th century, by means of the credit process and the manipulation of money, it has been gradually swallowing up the economic life. Finance constitutes a power above all States, from which the economies of all countries are controlled. One might also conjecture that, just as 20 years ago it was expedient for the forces of financial capitalism to bring about the fall of the USSR – which happened through a political agreement, unaided by revolution or violence – at this moment the need is arising to set up a world government raised above all the States, with none of them playing a dominant role, and that the political concept of statehood is giving way to that of world government, control of the issue of money being a fundamental step towards the realization of this goal. The most powerful and influential State, the U.S.A., may also need to disappear at the right moment. Or must, perhaps, a North American union first be constituted? Will the dollar have to be dropped and a new monetary system devised? In the modern world of finance and monetary movement, does money exist on such a high level that there is no reason to maintain its connection with the forces of the real economy?[14]

---

[14] Adrian Salbuchi – End of the United States, Beginning of World Government: "Especially relevant in this connection is an article published on 8th December 2008 in one of the most important and influential mouthpieces of the New World Order, the London daily 'The Financial Times', the title of which says it all: "And now for World Government". In it, the author tries to explain the need for cooperation between the nations so that certain global problems can be tackled, and he says that this needs to be done via institutions with characteristics similar to those of a planetary State, underpinned by a body of laws that also applies world-wide. The main antecedent taken is the neighbouring European Union which today unites 27 national States under a body of shared institutions: currency, laws, regulations, armed forces, Supreme Court, etc.

The reasons cited by the FT editor, Gideon Rachman, focus on three global problems which require global solutions: 1. The global financial crisis, 2. Global warming, and 3. "Global terrorism". One might mention that these three "global problems" pointed out by the FT can trace their origins directly or indirectly to the industrialized nations themselves and their structures of private power, which are trying today to "combat" them via global institutions governed by the same leading bodies.

In truth, the "global financial crisis" arose because of the fact that there has been imposed on the entire world a financial system that is absolutely irrational, unsustainable, and corrupt, driven by the markets of New York, London, Frankfurt, Paris and other places; "global warming" would be a product of the intensive, rash and irresponsible use of industrial methodologies and processes in the developed world and, via its mega-corporations, in other countries of the world, which can always reckon on the support of institutions like the World Bank and IMF and the collaboration of the ubiquitous "international investors" whose sole aim has been to maximize gains and profits to an insane level. And, finally, the much-trumpeted "war against global Islamic terrorism" is questioned today by wide and growing sections of world opinion, who believe that the real instigators, planners – and executors – of the major attacks of 9-11 in New York and Washington, of 7th July 2005 in London, of 11th March 2006 in Madrid; those in Bali, Bombay, etc. – including those on the AMIA headquarters and the Israeli Embassy in Buenos Aires – are probably attributable to a highly complex network of intelligence, counter-intelligence, front organizations, financiers and other covert, semi-covert, integrated and underground entities within the military, governing and intelligence structures themselves. These attacks defy the absurd and simplistic explanations asserting that they were perpetrated by "fundamentalist Islamic terrorists" who, in the cases where they were involved, were certainly cannon fodder and useful idiots who helped to give credence to the official versions. These were suitably sanitized and then propagated ad nauseam by the global multi-media, which form a part of this same New World Order structure; with which the circle closes and the serpent – like the ouroboros of mythology – bites its own tail."

4. Some Events of the 20th Century. The Ascendancy of Finance over Economy and Politics

Let us make a summary of the many facts which illustrate the process whereby the economic life absorbed the political life and finance absorbed the economy, during the 20th century. Many of them are well known because of the extremely wide diffusion of the Zeitgeist Video on You Tube, among many other sources. Today we need to regard States as companies in which the president functions as general manager, the ministers direct the various departments, and then the following questions arise: Who are the proprietors or shareholders? In what meetings do they decide what instructions have to be conveyed in hushed tones to the executive bodies? The nation-state, and the healthy patriotic feelings for the well-being of the community, are things of the past. From the evolutionary point of view, nationality ought to be superseded by human connections in a global world. But as the process of individual evolution is slow, the proprietors of the enterprises raised above the State use retardatively the primitive feelings of nationality, both within a country to excite the civil conflicts which they need for their purposes and between neighbouring countries, always applying the ancient formula of 'divide and rule', in addition to the international conflicts which also serve their ends.

The facts to which we refer centre, ultimately, around the act of deception that took place in 1913 with the assigning to the Federal Reserve of the United States the right to issue the dollar. The central bank independent of the government constituted itself from this moment as a quasi-private entity subject to minimal control from the Treasury Department of the U.S.A. or from the government's ministry for the economy. The aim of its point-by-point clarification here is to arrive at an understanding of the concept of credit, a concept on which money is based at the present time, its evolutionary character in relation to the trust or confidence which it implies, and also its counterpart in uncontrolled egoism, the principle that determines, unjustifiably, the use of credit in the world of finance.

In 1907 there was a run on the banks in the U.S.A., prompted by a rumour of insolvency of a New York bank that had been deliberately spread by J.P. Morgan, one of the big international bankers, who had much to gain from such an upheaval. A run of this kind, in which people withdrew their savings and the banks therefore recalled the loans from their clients, was the spark which not long afterwards, in 1913, would be used for the setting up of a single central bank independent of the government for the alleged purpose of stabilizing the issue of money. The biased investigation into what had happened in 1907 was entrusted to Nelson Aldrich, a man close to the banking cartels, and finally, during a secret meeting with 10 participants on Jekyll Island off the coast of Georgia, the formation was agreed and the Federal Reserve Act was signed. After a vote in the American Congress – cunningly arranged for a day on which there would be few congressmen present – on Christmas Eve 1913 President Woodrow Wilson ratified the corresponding law, and in this way management of the currency of the State that would quickly become the world's biggest economy, was given over to the Federal Reserve, or FED[15].

---

[15] Hodgson Brown, Hellen – The Web of Debt – Introduction – Captured by the Debt Spider - Fifth Edition January 2012:
"The following chapters track the web of deceit that has engulfed us in debt, and present a simple solution that could make the country solvent once again. It is not a new solution but dates back to the Constitution: the power to create money needs to be returned to the government and the people it represents. The federal debt could be paid, income taxes could be eliminated, and social programs could be expanded; and this could all be done *without* imposing austerity measures on the people or sparking runaway inflation. Utopian as that may sound, it represents the thinking of some of America's brightest and best, historical and contemporary, including Abraham Lincoln, Thomas Jefferson and Benjamin Franklin. Among other arresting facts explored in this book are that:
- The "Federal" Reserve is not actually federal. It is a private corporation owned by a consortium of very large multinational banks. (Chapter 13)
- Except for coins, the government does not create money. Dollar bills (Federal Reserve Notes) are created by the private Federal Reserve, which *lends* them to the banks that lend them to the government, individuals and businesses. (Chapter 2)
- Tangible currency (coins and dollar bills) together make up less than 3 percent of the U.S. money supply. The other 97 percent exists only as data entries on computer screens, and *all* of this money was created by banks in the form of loans. (Chapters 2 and 17)
- The money that banks lend is not recycled from pre-existing deposits. It is new money, which did not exist until it was lent. (Chapters 17 and 18)

The FED is, strictly speaking, a private banking corporation which, once its board of directors has been elected, is not accountable to anyone and is not subject to an auditing process. The organization is directed by a Board of Governors of 7 members and a Federal Open Market Committee consisting of these 7, plus 5 representatives of 12 federal banks of some of the states of the U.S.A. The seven governors, who are those who take the decisions, are banking experts nominated by the President and approved by Congress, occupy the post for the unbelievably long period of 14 years, and even longer in the case of the post of president and vice-president (Alan Greenspan remained from 1987 to 2006). The pretext for such a lengthy mandate is to ensure independence from the swings of political change, as the monarchies

---

- Thirty percent of the money created by banks with accounting entries is *invested for their own accounts.* (Chapter 18)
- The American banking system, which at one time extended productive loans to agriculture and industry, has today become a giant betting machine. An estimated *$370 trillion* are now riding on complex high-risk bets known as derivatives – 28 times the $13 trillion annual output of the entire U.S. economy. These bets are funded by big U.S. banks and are made largely with borrowed money created on a computer screen. Derivatives can be and have been used to manipulate markets, loot businesses, and destroy competitor economies. (Chapters 20 and 32)
- The U.S. federal debt has not been paid off since the days of Andrew Jackson. Only the interest gets paid, while the principal portion continues to grow. (Chapter 2)
- The federal income tax was instituted specifically to coerce taxpayers to pay the interest due to the banks on the federal debt. If the money supply had been created by the government rather than borrowed from banks that created it, the income tax would have been unnecessary. (Chapters 13 and 43)
- The interest alone on the federal debt will soon be more than the taxpayers can afford to pay. When we can't pay, the Federal Reserve's debt-based dollar system must collapse. (Chapter 29)
- Contrary to popular belief, creeping inflation is not caused by the government irresponsibly printing dollars. It is caused by banks expanding the money supply with loans. (Chapter 10)
- Most of the runaway inflation seen in "banana republics" has been caused, not by national governments printing money for the nation's needs, but by global institutional speculators attacking local currencies and devaluing them on international markets. (Chapter 25)
- The same sort of speculative devaluation could happen to the U.S. dollar if international investors were to abandon it as a global "reserve" currency, something they are now threatening to do in retaliation for what they perceive to be American economic imperialism. (Chapters 29 and 37)
- There is a way out of this morass. The early American colonists found it, and so did Abraham Lincoln and some other national leaders: the government can take back the money-issuing power from the banks. (Chapters 8 and 24)."

once did in Europe. To sum up – the entire management of the currency depends on lobbying and on the pressure exerted by the representatives of capital. The representatives are selected every so often (that is to say, after very long periods of time) by the President first and the democratic authorities afterwards. What is more, the U.S. Government draws money on loan from the FED and pays it the corresponding interest; for every dollar needed to cover the nation's budget, a debt accumulates which has to be paid by the taxpayer and if what is collected is not enough, the FED is authorized to print more money, which also will be lent out so that the debt can be paid, which in the end the citizens will pay with more taxes. Each dollar issued by the FED is loaned to the Government, and interest is charged which steadily accumulates, since the creators of money take precautions to ensure that what is loaned is never enough to cover the total of the nation's budget and that it is still less possible through payment received from taxation for all that has been loaned to be repaid.

The intention at the beginning of the 1960's of President John Fitzgerald Kennedy to regain State control over the issue of money and bring reform to the system through introduction of a silver standard, was the reason behind his assassination in Dallas in 1963. But this is nothing new, since the struggle of the great men who forged the independence of the United States, for example, Benjamin Franklin (1706-1790), was signalized by the will to free themselves from the domination, at that time, by the interests of British capital. As he is quoted in the film Zeitgeist, Thomas Jefferson (President from 1801-1809) said: "I believe that banking institutions are more dangerous to our liberties than standing armies. If the American people ever allow private banks to control the issue of their currency, first by inflation, then by deflation, the banks and corporations that will grow up around [the banks] will deprive the people of all property until their children wake-up homeless on the continent their fathers conquered. The issuing power should be taken from the banks and restored to the people, to whom it properly belongs." President Andrew Jackson (presidency from 1829-1837) also had strong words to describe the activity of the banking cartel: "a hydra-headed monster eating the flesh of the common man."[16] And finally, another assassination of emblematic significance was that of Abraham Lincoln (President from 1861-1865) when, during the Civil War, he reclaimed control of the issue of money,

---

[16] Hodgson Brown, Hellen – The Web of Debt – Third Millenium Press.

just as had been done in the colonial beginnings with respect to British capital.

From 1913 onwards there began to circulate the dogma of the central banks' need for independence, which was also exported to all other countries, making it impossible for the U.S. Congress to regain control of the issue of the dollar.

From then onwards the FED brought about various movements entailing periods of plentiful supply and then withdrawal of money in circulation (boom and crash), which enabled it to organize "scientifically" – as it was expressed in 1920 by Charles Lindbergh, a Congressman opposed to the banking cartel – other runs on banks, both in 1920 after the First World War, and in 1929. These crashes had as a consequence, on both occasions, the collapse of small banks and the consolidation of the financial cartel of the 5 or 6 great fortunes of the world (Rockefeller, Warburg, Rothschild, Morgan and a few others). Of course, in these periods of abundance the gains were privatized and in the periods of restriction the losses were socialized, in a conceptual oscillation between support of the theories of economic liberalism of Adam Smith and the theories of State interventionism upheld by John Maynard Keynes. This is an oscillation that has nothing to do with thought, but is a matter of pure convenience disguised as the difficulties which the "economic sciences" seemingly present. This became clear in the crisis of 2008 in which, after years of preaching economic liberalism, from one day to the next there was a switch to the State interventionism that is prepared to rescue those who are leaders of the greater State that is raised above all states.

Up until the year 1913 the need to provide backing for currency in gold was the standard for all countries, and each country did this as it was able according to its resources, a difference that regulated currency values. But from the 1929 crisis onwards, when the U.S.A. could no longer back up the dollar with gold, the struggle began for the accumulation of all stocks of the metal on the part of the FED, culminating in the extreme measure of confiscating all citizens' gold in 1933. The advance in the direction of World War II was also – the financial cartels being fully aware that, for them, there is no better business than war – prompted by the indebtedness of the nations that would result from it. The dependent companies had no qualms about financing the Bolshevism of Lenin (electrification of the whole countryside in Russia) in 1917, and also the formation and the rise of Nazism for the purpose of stealthily confronting both bandits, Hitler and Stalin, at the bloodiest moment of the Second War and putting an end to the threat of a possible Eurasia. "Mother, I bow down before gold... money is a powerful knight" (Francisco Quevedo); there is no doubt that this is how the system works. The financial élites are building up experience in the business of being the only creators of money and of lending it at interest, determining the rise and fall of prices, using wars as tools, since it is much more profitable than work in politics and in the real economy.

Another quotation from the book of Hodgson Brown: "The international bankers have succeeded in doing more than just controlling the money supply. Today they actually create the money supply, while making it appear to be created by the government. This devious scheme was revealed by Sir Josiah Stamp, director of the Bank of England and the second richest man in Britain in the 1920s. Speaking at the University of Texas in 1927, he dropped this bombshell: *"The modern banking system manufactures money out of nothing. The process is perhaps the most astounding piece of sleight of hand that was ever invented. Banking was conceived in inequity and born in sin . . . . Bankers own the earth. Take it away from them but leave them the power to create money, and, with a flick of a pen, they will create enough money to buy it back again. . . . Take this great power away from them and all great fortunes like mine will disappear, for then this would be a better and happier world to live in. . . . But, if you want to continue to be the slaves of bankers and pay the cost of your own slavery, then let bankers continue to create money and control credit'.*"[17]

The U.S.A. entered the Second War through the fraud of the attack on Pearl Harbour when, after pursuing the Japanese to the very limit, they found in the attack the pretext for entering the war. At its conclusion, the U.S.A. was the country that was hoarding more than 60% of the world's gold reserves, enabling its currency to establish a parameter on this basis. In the Bretton Woods accords of 1944 an equivalence was fixed, of US$35 per ounce of gold. Thus the gold standard was set up for the dollar only, and the dollar standard – which was more flexible than gold and in addition drew interest – for all other countries, which therefore began to use the dollar as their reserve currency. The 'Golden Age', the illusion of possible unlimited economic growth, lasted from 1945 to 1970, and it became ever clearer to the FED that, the more

---

[17] Hodgson Brown, Hellen – The Web of Debt – Introduction – Captured by the Debt Spider – Fifth Edition January 2012.

44

dollars they issued and loaned, the more influence they would have in the world, and the less involved they would need to be in the arduous labour of the real economy. As a reserve currency, the debt of other countries was the credit of the U.S.A., and this form of accumulation, combined with and by means of control of the U.S. Government, was far more profitable than the honest striving for economic surplus. The question of leverage began to intensify – how to extend the lever of gain by acquiring more money on loan, boosting the issue of money through its influence on the successive scale of investments.

If a bank of another country issues money, the increasing amount in circulation and the contrast with the dollar as reserve currency triggers a devaluation of the local currency and a wave of inflation. But this does not happen with the dollar, as it has been transformed into the reserve currency of all other countries (more than 70% of central banks in the world hold reserves in dollars, only 15% in euros and a tiny percentage in gold). The businesses of other countries, which export to the U.S.A. – for example, the manufacturers of cars or foods – charge for their sales in dollars and, when they exchange them in their own country for the local currency, the central bank in question increases its dollar reserves, which is why the policy of many nations is to encourage exports paid for in dollars. Then, to obtain interest on these reserves, the countries began to buy U.S. Treasury bonds which, in their turn, are issued in great quantities for payment of their debt with the FED and, as they are addicted to consumption and maintain a standard of living higher than is warranted by their real capacities, they are also addicted to receiving money on loan. Since the dollar is the currency of reserve in the central banks of different countries, it does not produce inflation in the U.S.A. and the FED can carry on with the usury of the continuous issue of dollars and the collection of the interest due.

At the beginning of the 70's it was obvious that they had been corrupted by the issue of dollars, and so, in 1971, it was decided to "deregulate the financial market", whereby Nixon suspended the convertibility of the dollar into gold, devaluing it by only 10%, and starting from this moment to provide backing to the dollar through "armed diplomacy" alone. The beginning of the decade also saw the first two big crises due to increase in the price of oil, and the question continues to be asked, whether they were not provoked by the financial élites themselves. This was also implied in declarations of Kissinger to the effect that the oil-producing countries should receive more dollars for their oil so that they could pay the debts arising from the import of technology from the U.S.A. The need to pay much more for the oil would allow the issue of more dollars and extension of the vicious circle of gain arising from the interest due, in addition to payment of the debts of the oil-producing countries, and in this way the money would remain within their coffers (going out, and then coming back increased in volume).

After Nixon´s decision – between 1970 and 2001 – the uncontrolled issue of money expanded by 2000% without backing in gold, beginning the period of flotation of monetary values relative to the dollar and in contrast to the violence of its imposition by "diplomatic" means or through armed force, with the intervention of the international organizations. For example, it grows ever clearer that the intention of Saddam Hussein to accept euros for oil was a decisive factor in the war against Iraq. The violence in the Middle East continues to be related to the prohibition of trade in oil with any other currency than the dollar.

If we ask how to connect the U.S. trade deficit with the dollar system, the answer is simple: you sink into debt through over-consumption, and then restore balance through the sale of money. If we ask how they have managed to get this way of conducting business accepted by other countries, we need only consider the theme of the power imbalance, supported by arms and violence, since the Second World War. One is not allowed to cast doubt on "confidence" in the mission of the U.S.A. as defenders of the free world and democracy. The issue of money was given over to the whim and the need for accumulation imposed by the FED in its negotiations and its manipulation of the U.S. Treasury Department – that is to say: before the eyes of the world the armed diplomacy standard of the dollar has been established with no other backing than this. At the same time, thanks to the philosophy of "shop until you drop", with the aim of keeping the economy going, the internal debt of the citizens is growing continually and, combined with the external debt, the total debt of the U.S.A. has exploded with the bubble of the mortgage loans. The economy has stagnated, investment is made in China, as capital shows no national loyalty, and unemployment grows, destroying the middle class.

But the coffers of many countries, above all, those of the menacing China, are overflowing with dollars; there is a growing number of countries who have awakened to the fraud on which the dollar system has been constructed, and with the crisis of 2008 the heroic deed began of digging an ever-deepening pit in the same fateful direction. The "dolorous plight" of the dollar – 'el dolor del dólar'.

The process of globalization since the fall of the Berlin Wall has brought with it world-wide dollarization and investment by countries in the hidden debt of the U.S.A. The countries with a bigger trade surplus – China, Japan, Canada, Mexico and Germany – which accumulate their reserves in dollars, are the main creditors of the U.S.A. because *"What is perverse about this system is the fact that Washington has succeeded in getting foreign surplus countries to invest their own savings, to be a creditor to the US, buying Treasury Bonds."*[18] The debts of the U.S.A. are the assets of the rest of the world, and the international system functions in a vicious circle from which it is difficult to imagine an escape, apart from the collapse of the whole international financial and economic system. This is the reason why the countries continue to buy debt, and the U.S.A. acts as though the system of issuing money could go on for ever. But the countries with a big trade surplus, like China and Japan (the position of the European Union towards its partners in the far West to whom it has been annexed irreversibly since the War, in the European-Atlantic pact, is ambiguous) are questioning the perverse nature of such a system. If one looks around for alternatives, the menacing and much-feared Eurasia comes to view. With the latest crisis, this situation seems to have reached a limit, and the countries with reserves may decide to diversify them. The question is, what sort of agreement is reached between them, particularly where Russia and China are concerned, and what are the interests of the financial élite on their way to a world government?

The poor countries with their big external debt cannot do very much because, according to the methodology applied to them, their élites are influenced to ensure that the central banks concerned continue to issue less money than is needed to cover the State budget, so that they have to ask for loans and see themselves obliged to constantly devalue their currency, to sell their key industries and pay their external debt in dollars to the U.S.A. The countries that have the possibility of working towards a sustainability of their own, and which, from the economic point of view, would be in a position to take the steps needed to bring about a new social order, do not have the necessary cultural basis – that is, awareness in their citizens – and their intellectual classes are continually crushed, or corrupted by means of money.

With the present crisis and the enormous amount of money that has been issued for the rescue of banks, businesses, insurers and countries –

---

[18] F. William Engdahl – The Dollar System and US economic reality post-Iraq War – Remarks in Feldkirch, Austria, September 2003.

that is, the attempt to resolve the problem through applying the very remedy that caused the sickness – we have arrived at a terminal stage and the question is, how much longer the patient can expect to live. We can ask whether the increasing severity of this crisis is not being provoked so that the necessity can arise for a world government and a single central bank. Perhaps with stages in between? The wish to set up a world government has been expressed on various occasions by the system representatives themselves.

One of the steps in this direction which was discussed at the G20 meeting in April 2009, was the idea of reviving the so-called Special Drawing Rights (SDR's), a type of money that was put into circulation and which the International Monetary Fund (IMF) has issued since 1970, just before the oil crises, but which has so far hardly ever been used. This money is in the hands of the central banks of the countries belonging to the Fund, which allocated it to each country as new reserves on the strength of its existing reserves, but granting twice as much of these SDR's to a country in exchange for its provision of real money to help to finance the system. This type of money is there to be used in case of need among the member countries, and if more than 30% is spent, they are obliged to replace it using other reserves. The U.S.A. has run out of gold ingots of 1 kg., that is to say, it can no longer fulfil the contracts denominated in this unit, at the same time as, in China, gold reserves have doubled since 2003. The SDR's were a first attempt to create a reserve asset that would not be convertible to gold – before Nixon's decision – and now the wish is to use them in the manner of canasta (in dollars, pounds, euros and yen) with the aim of creating a value that will begin to circulate in the trade system. That is, a step brought about by the IMF towards the creation of an international currency, which is not based on a standard but rather on the decision of its makers. The steps that are taken towards the formation of a world central bank have to be very gradual so that they do not cause popular revolt or civil disorder, but they are happening at a time when there is an attempt to distract and alarm people with other issues, for example, swine flu.

The financial hegemony of the U.S.A. over the distorted dollar system increasingly depends upon the support of the rest of the world to sustain American debt, and this is more and more difficult to achieve. The vulnerability of the debt therefore drives them to an increasingly unilateral policy and to aggression as an external policy aimed at maintaining the monopoly of the world's oil supplies as the only way of escape.

Strictly speaking, there are 5 big banks that have failed and hold the greatest debt (J.P. Morgan Chase, Bank of America, Citybank, Goldman Sachs, Wells Fargo Wachovia and HSBC Bank U.S.A.), which turn out to be, themselves, owners of the FED.

5. From Barter Economy to Monetary Economy to Credit Economy

Barter can only exist in a small community living in a limited geographical space. The relative value of this product or that is determined by the need for it – that is, by what value a specific object has for somebody. This, seen from a higher perspective, represents the law of supply and demand that there is for a given product. But the concepts of supply and demand within barter economy are limited because, here, we are on a level of valuation that is very concrete and particular. Although it is true that when a thing has much value for someone, but he can easily acquire it, he will value it less than if it is very difficult to obtain – in barter economy supply and demand are, generally not comparable, as they are bound up with the enclosed relations between people.

Regarding the concept of value, let us return to what was expressed earlier – namely, that not only material or tangible things, but also cultural or intangible things have a value. The concept of value is different from that of price, though both have to be expressed in terms of money so that it does not become abstract. From the pole of nature or the physical body we speak of the value attached to the production of commodities. From the pole of the spirit, of the value attached to a creation based in the application of human capacities. The comparison and mutual compensation of tangible and intangible values, that is, the criteria that are applied in society, are extremely complex, and the imbalance between the cultural (spiritual) and material economic poles will continue to worsen to the extent that the advance continues of the materialistic society of the last few centuries, which more and more devalues spiritual work.

The passage through the material, physical aspect has been an evolutionary necessity for science and must be understood as a time for a strengthening of the objectivity of thought. The limit has, however, already been crossed, the most convincing proof of this being the appalling social Darwinism that holds sway everywhere, the survival of the fittest. As the cultural life was being absorbed and contaminated by politics and economy, with scarcely any cultural sector existing independently of the economic life, society suffered increasingly from the absence of input from the cultural-spiritual sector, and we do not develop an awareness of the needs on this level, or we sacrifice them, motivated by fear and by the insistence on the need for excessive consumption. We have to do here with a macro-social reflection of the weakness of thought-activity in the individual human being.

As money was coming to be used more for the purpose of objectivizing commercial interchange, the individual's need to attach a value to things became less personal, more abstract, and in the market, as a consequence, the concept of supply and demand began to predominate over personal evaluation. But as compared to barter, the monetary economy brought with it a huge advantage: the freedom in space and time, which was leading towards the experience of unity on a globalized Earth – a symptom of the need to be conscious also of the experience of spiritual unity, and how to attain it.

The lack of direct experience with regard to the value of things when they were not being exchanged, but purchased, made it necessary to find a standard for the value of the currency in use. Initially, this standard was wheat, as it is on the one hand an archetype of the basic human need for food and, on the other, the grain of wheat is sufficiently stable in size and in perishability to be able to serve as a unit of measurement and of backing for currency. On the level of material needs, money based on the wheat standard refers to the annual production of a given area of square metres of this cereal. On the understanding that processes always occur simultaneously and in sequence, grain gave way to gold as the standard, since gold was always regarded as the most stable value for comparison[19].

Then there was a shift to the banking system (controlled by the State), which issues paper money with a backing in gold – that is, with the promise to pay a stipulated amount in gold for the banknotes issued. The significance of gold as an exchange currency is far less easily definable than the value of wheat; it has to do with a legal agreement between human beings, since it is not possible to establish a criterion of need or of production. All the metals are an expression of the planetary

[19] See Budd, Christopher Houghton – Of Wheat and Gold – New Economy Publications – 1996.

processes held back in space and time and refracted in the Earth, whereby gold is the representative of the Sun process on the Earth.

In esoteric Christianity the Sun represents Christ, the equilibrium in the human soul between the forces of body and spirit, and it is held that, since his incarnation in the 1st century, he is to be found, no longer on the Sun, but on the Earth itself. The implication of this and of all that has been said so far, is that, on the one hand, the responsibility for the evolution of nature itself is placed in the hands of man himself – or, in other words, it depends upon man whether the plants can continue to grow. And, on the other hand, it is necessary for the human being while he is living on the Earth to raise his consciousness to the plane from which life originates.

Gold is the most difficult metal to find, as metal, in a mine or a seam, but the reverse side of this is that it can ultimately be found in dilution, distributed everywhere almost uniformly. And it is precisely because of this diluted form in which it occurs, that it is impossible for anyone to take possession of all the gold that exists. Is this just a coincidence? One could say that we all breathe-in gold in the atmosphere and, in the threefold organization of man, this is closely connected to the central part of the human being. On the soul level this relates to the feelings that arise from his 'I', and, on the physiological level, to the heart.

The significance of gold is closely bound up with the evolution of consciousness, and we have already referred to the intentions underlying the work of the Knights Templar. In the Renaissance, when the scientific spirit was born, the alchemists saw a parallel between the process of transforming the metals into gold, and the inner moral process. Today the spiritual value associated to it – expressed, for example, in the crown of the medieval monarch or in the idea of spiritual transformation upheld by the alchemists – is confused with the commercial value attached to it as man advanced towards materialism. The gold standard emerged in the economy in the 18th century, with Sir Isaac Newton the master of the emission. This happened at a moment when burgeoning industry was causing merchandise and money to separate from one another, for the sake of an advance towards a world economy. The wheat standard ceased to be applied after the defeat of Napoleon. However, gold does not lose its value; in times of crisis man takes refuge again and again in gold, because he ascribes to it an eternal value, enabling it to serve as a thermometer for the economy: when gold rises, the dollar sinks, and vice-versa.

One could say that wheat and gold represent the forces of the human body and soul, since both substances, although of absolutely different quality, are material. This material element is not sufficient for an understanding of the meaning of money, and it is possible that at least three elements are needed if we are to get them to correspond to physical, soul and spiritual needs.

At a third stage of evolution, it was finally necessary for spiritual needs to express themselves, and we now move on to the credit-based economy which, as its name suggests, is recognition of the human capacity to undertake and realize a noble goal which gives us confidence that it deserves to be financed. The development of credit and the development of the human consciousness which was emancipating itself from nature, are parallel processes. Here we can imagine a polarity between the economy of the Earth and that of credit, two aspects of an inseparable unity existing in the tension between body and spirit that is experienced more or less consciously by the human being on Earth.

More or less evolved stages of consciousness are elements that vary from nation to nation, since they are closely bound up with the history and the telluric forces of different regions, but in our epoch it is essentially an individual matter. This can be seen in cosmopolitanism and in the migrations that it implies, and both in globalization and in the process of free individualization which we are going through today. The possibility of credit arises because human capacities have evolved, and they are the very factor that has enabled the accumulation of capital to come about, for the purpose of lending. But as soon as there is less need of loans for increase in production, it is possible to place confidence in such capacities for the more efficient undertaking of new activities that will create spiritual values. These contribute to the process whereby cultural-spiritual development is made accessible to all human beings.

Credit economy has its spiritual basis in the trust placed by one human being in another; originally, money was loaned without interest, as the Church regarded lending with interest as usury. Viewed conceptually, interest replaces confidence in the reciprocity of mutual aid – you today, myself tomorrow – and offers, instead, the advantage of profit. That is to say, it replaces the lender's confidence that the money will be repaid or loaned to him if he needs it on a future occasion, with a security resting on a legal basis. Strictly speaking, interest has been so far a necessity for social growth due to the complexity of human relations; and, with the legalization of credit, human relations themselves are freed from dependency and are able to widen.

There are two stages in the process of capital accumulation which tends in the direction of credit. The first is the moment when all that is accumulated is reinvested in production or is loaned out for a new investment in the economic process, with the interest received being transformed into capital that is used in the same way – i.e. the production of commodities. This stage consists in the healthy growth of what is needed by production to make it more efficient, and thus to make life in general more comfortable. Through the application of capacities to social organization and the building of machines, human energy is saved, which can be expended for the satisfaction of other needs of the human being. Credit money accumulated and channelled into production gave rise to industry. A machine that allows work to be done more efficiently is, initially, the result of the individual capacity of this machine's inventor. Undoubtedly, up to a certain moment the fruits of this inventive talent remain in the hands of the inventor, but they soon pass into the hands of the industrial producer, thus providing him with the capital that enables him to manufacture, perfect and multiply the invention. Given the diversity of capacities we human beings possess, the inventor possibly goes on to think of a new invention, and not of ways of obtaining economic advantage from the previous one, as it is a realm that corresponds more to the economy than to creation in the strict sense. There are different capacities which distinguish spiritual workers from economic workers.

A second stage arises when the productive need has been or is considered satisfied and the profit gained thanks to the initial investment of capital does not need to be reinvested in economic production, but forms a capital surplus. This is a crucial point in the history of the economic life, a moment when the surplus arising from the productive process is not reinvested in it, but is used for new loans with interest, thanks to the abstract value attached to money. At this moment, money severs itself from the economic process that brought it into being, and if a good destiny does not guide the surplus into proper channels, it enters the financial process of purchase and sale of money, or usury.

When finance begins, the money generated by the trade in interest loses all connection with what it originated from, and it transforms itself into a product in its own right. But the supply of money cannot be regarded only as a benefit, in view of the fact that, as we have seen, its function is as a regulator and not a creator of values, and only the functions that create values, tangible or intangible, can legitimately acquire the benefits gained. According to Rudolf Steiner, the problem lies in the fact that, relative to any other product, a plus has been granted to money, since it does not grow old, does not wear out, is not consumed like other things that are sold in the world – food, a car, to name a few examples – but, on the contrary, it increases in value through the payment of interest. This "perversion", meaning this corrupted version of what is necessary in a healthy social process, comes about when the economy develops to the point where more money has been made than is needed for the functioning of the economy itself. The surplus may be real – in which case we are dealing with a healthy profit – or it may be an estimate made by those who are managing the money (whereby the correct estimation may have been confused due to an incorrect distribution of the gains among the members of the company in question).

When money flows towards the economic process there is always a devaluation, because the commodities are consumed or undergo a depreciation; but when trading in money begins – finance, or the sale of money with interest on the interest (compound interest) – this gains an unfair advantage over other commodities because, in not losing its value, its reproduction adds up. We are dealing here with the modern version of usury. Lending at a fair rate of interest (to cover administrative and banking costs for doing the practical work) is a necessity of the modern world and its complex global relations. Initially, banks did not create credit money, but drew it from the surplus arising from the economic process. When the process of finance began, the distortion arose, whereby money was being created for its own sake, thus leading the economic-financial life to its destruction. An abstract illusion which throws a veil over reality, but from which some of us are beginning to awaken, as we learn the lessons of the successive crises.

The point at which the economy no longer needs funds to reinvest in production and there is saturation of money, gives evidence of the level of evolution that has enabled individual capacities to be brought to bear in practical life. Can one see here a symptom of the need for development of human consciousness on a purely cultural-spiritual level? Because it is one thing to develop the rational, inventive intelligence for the creation of machines and technical devices that facilitate practical life, and it is quite another thing to develop spiritually in the fields of scientific knowledge, the arts and religion.

Practical inventiveness which, after crossing a certain limit, produces environmental devastation such as we are experiencing everywhere today, needs a parallel development of spiritual awareness of man's belonging to the Earth and to the cosmos. The maturing of the consciousness we have attained causes crisis in the economy and requires us to be able to understand the process – an awakening to the new that is happening in our epoch.

If human labour is so fruitful that it continues to generate surpluses of money, which is equivalent to an excess of production, and the level of need for the production and consumption of commodities has been exceeded, the accumulated capital has to flow in other directions. Strictly speaking, there are three or four directions in which it can flow.

The first and the second, representing single options that would further development and are, in principle, adopted in reciprocal relation to one another, are that the State should legislate so that the flow of capital would be more equitable in its distribution and could attempt to repair the immense damage resulting from human egoism. The State can fulfil this function through a proper use of the money received from the labour of its citizens, which comes to expression in the payment of taxes. Payment of taxes could come to be regarded as a compulsory donation regulated by the State with the aim of realizing a certain level of equality in the distribution of profits gained. A flow of this kind has been implemented by the European welfare states since the Second World War, but due to the increasing engulfment of the political by the economic sector, its moral limitations have grown more and more evident. An economy that absorbs politics imposes on it the moral direction of its own educational and health policies. The individual who strives for freedom is ever more strongly opposed to a determination of his cultural life by the State. Payment of taxes is not done voluntarily, because so long as the political system sells itself to the economic system, the individual will not gladly hand over his money to the State.

The second option is that the surplus should flow as a voluntary donation from the economic sector towards the free unfolding of culture. In reality, the cultural and economic sectors have to join together, because the only thing that can bring about a fairer distribution of money – through an awakening of empathy with the lives of our fellow human beings – is the development of a cultural pole whose freedom is guaranteed by the political State, and which can radiate a spiritual influence into the surrounding world. One cannot oblige anyone to be good or generous – this is something that is freely decided upon – and the forces of the ideal of brotherhood in the economy, and also those of equality and fairness in the political life, can only radiate out from the freedom of the cultural sector. This means that the problem of fair distribution – to meet the needs of those who, for whatever reason, cannot earn a living – although realization of the ideal of equality which ensures the dignity of all citizens depends upon the State, rests ultimately on the social forces freely cultivated by the individual in the cultural sphere. When a law is made a loophole can always be found, because wrong will inevitably be done when voluntary giving is replaced by compulsory taxation, as we no longer live in an epoch in which moral conduct can be regulated by Roman law. In the modern world the necessity grows ever more evident – however difficult it may seem, to make steps in this direction – for the ideal of equality in the political life and brotherhood in the economic life. These ideals are formed – and one can aspire towards them – under the spiritual influence of the free cultural life. No-one can be forced to be good, generous or compassionate.

The cultural sector, as we indicated above, is a sector that is in need of capital because of the fact that it consumes but does not produce material goods, and steps must therefore be taken to correct the imbalance that arose from the difficulty in evaluating spiritual goods in the course of our evolution. The imbalance appears in the history of the evolution of human consciousness through our loss of a direct link with the spiritual world and of the ability to recognize the capacities of our fellow human beings. This symptom is most acute in the most modern societies. The institutionalized dogma of traditional churches does not, in general, satisfy spiritual needs, and the human being experiences how necessary, and how difficult, it is to re-establish this link out of his own forces, and is therefore eager to find whatever will restore to him his true dignity.

The need for funding for the free spiritual life, whether for individuals, institutions, colleges or universities etc. – that is, for the realms of science, art and religion – has always been recognized by human society, and in the medieval period the Church had the responsibility for encouraging donations and carrying out the distribution. Then, when the State was at its zenith from the French Revolution onwards – and even today in some welfare states particularly in Central and Northern Europe – enough money is acquired for the State to be able to finance education and health by way of taxation. But even then we can see more and more, how harmful it is for culture to be dependent on the political State, and increasingly at the mercy of the economic interests and pressures to which the State is subject. Liberalization of the economy, absorption of the economic by the financial sector, means an ever-diminishing flow of capital towards culture, which is thus conditioned and bound to the will of the élite for the management of "culture" – which is made use of for the furthering of their aims. Educational content or health projects are given a particular orientation – that of the economic interests – depriving individuals of their spiritual freedom when it comes to voting. States have become servants of the interests of capital on the public level. In the private sector's link with economic gain, for example, via the predominance of medical laboratories and the chemical industry over an objective consideration of health needs and the freedom to bring them to awareness in thinking, we see yet another emerging, clear symptom of the general lack of ethics and morality.

Unfortunately, in the modern world two outmoded ways of using surplus capital continue to be applied. One is war, which brings in profit from the sale of armaments. In wars the destruction takes place of what the economic process has generated, and one can ask whether the so-called "reconstruction" of the areas affected does not form a part of this modus operandi. May the following suffice for the present. In her book 'The Shock Doctrine', Naomi Klein asks the question in connection with the hair-raising reality of the destructive machinations of the usurpers of this surplus capital. What she calls "shock doctrine" means that one takes advantage of the disorientation, chaos and weakness of citizens, following upon a catastrophe, whether natural or provoked, in order to apply in the "reconstruction" economic doctrines and commercial plans which otherwise, with a stronger population, would be resisted. Milton Friedman, the father of economic market liberalism and guru of the Chicago Boys, put it like this: *"Only a crisis – real or perceived as such – can produce a real change, and when this crisis happens the actions that are taken depend on the ideas that are around."*

And fourthly, only in appearance more honest than war, there is the channelling of the surplus into the game of finance, taking possession of the machine for producing money as we described above, at the same time as, mendaciously, making the State responsible for the extensive issue of money and for inflation. On the intellectual level the strategy is to make over-complex the concepts of economy – as is done by many bad doctors in their profession when they use technical jargon in talking to patients susceptible to this approach – so that when it comes to understanding how the economy works, the difficulties are consigned to the exclusive world of the specialists, with the help and through control of the media. The financial sector ends up by using the State, of which it has basically taken possession by means of economic forces, as a scapegoat for all ills, war and inflation. State functionaries are no more than the external façade – which is changed politically whenever it grows unpopular – of a more powerful financial force behind the scenes, a kind of apolitical monarchy whose agents are the true holders of power in the world.

Just as the first two factors – redistribution by the State and the directing of money to culture through private donation – are interconnected, so also are the last two. For, war and destruction are, as we said, excellent ways of sustaining the financial system, through the loan of money to the States requiring armaments and through allowing the peoples who are divided into the various factions to tear each other apart in either internal or external conflict, according to the convenience of the members of the élite who take the decisions.

Usury, which is practised in finance through the countless instruments that have been created and have grown exponentially since 1970, does not properly belong to the world of economy. It is a perverted sector which, as such, does not belong to the archetypal triad – economic, political and cultural life – of a healthy social organism. Despite the accumulation of money that it produces, it works against the economy and destroys it, because the time effects of the quantity of money in circulation are concealed, bringing about inflation and the devaluation of national currencies. As we have seen, this devaluation does not happen to the dollar because, after the Second World War, the momentum of the indiscriminate advance of the Western forces has assumed the guise of international reserve currency, on the grounds that they were the victors.

6. The Surplus arising from Economic Production – Its True Value and Function

In Ch. 2 we discussed the parallel between the threefold structuring of society and the threefoldness of the individual human being, and we saw the correspondence of their parts within the whole. The human soul faculties – thinking, feeling and willing – have a relation to the social sectors of culture, politics and economy. When we think of this correlation we see that it is so complex that it can even be approached from opposite points of view to those presented, this being the richness of a conception that is not a dogma, but a framework that serves as a basis from which the subject can be illumined from various perspectives.

In the individual human being the work of self-knowledge begins with the awakening of the conscious pole in a thinking that is enlivened by the forces of one's own will. As the thought-activity develops through being imbued with will, this inspires an awakening of feelings oriented towards the spirit and thus arises the will to follow those impulses which lead to actions that correspond to the thoughts. To act in accordance with what we are able to think is still very difficult to achieve fully, given that thinking is difficult and doing is easy (as we see in the world all the time) – but to carry out what we think is still more difficult. The truth is, that we human beings – or the majority of us, at least – need to be fed, clothed and provided with a roof over our head, in order for thinking to unfold on our path to action. The problem of the chicken and the egg is insoluble in the absence of good-will, but there are, in fact, many people in the modern world whose basic needs are met by grace – that is, with little or no effort on their part. However, the difficulties experienced in the world today show that, of this group, there are few indeed who have been endowed by destiny with – apart from economic advantage – the spiritual capacities to contribute towards change. What are the limits of human desire, and how can it be self-regulating?

On the social level, the individual work of people who enjoy special conditions and capacities in the spiritual sphere will, in principle, have to promote the production and just distribution of what is required to meet physical needs. Following the principle that "man does not live by bread alone", it should be possible to compensate for the scarcity of resources through dedication on the cultural level and through sacrifice of certain material "necessities" which show themselves to be superfluous when a person feels nourished spiritually. In his book, 'Threefold Society', Rudolf Steiner says that the emergence of Bolshevist ideology in the middle of the 19th century, was due to the fact that the intellectuals, unaffected by the decline of working conditions in the early stages of industrialism, did not notice the emptiness and the spiritual need that arose among the proletariat, and tried to fill the void with ideas alone – the dialectical materialism of Marx – meaning that they tried to substitute spirituality with ideology. The unconscious or instinctive need on the basic physical level, which is met concretely with money for buying and selling, must be satisfied as a fundamental human right, on the level of equality. In the social realm it is essential that social policies should be implemented, which aim at the satisfaction of basic needs. As this affects the economic sphere it can, like the chicken and the egg, only be called for in a positive way, out of the surplus flowing from the spiritual life of a number of individuals. It is not a Marxist proposal we are putting forward here, and we are seeking equality on neither the economic nor the cultural, but only the political level, in which the State can and must, rightly, be involved.

Marx turned the epistemology of Hegel upside-down. One of the great philosophers of German Romanticism, Hegel described germinally and for the first time the inner dialectic between the 'I' and the content of what is consciously thought, as an inner duality which is reproduced in the soul that observes itself and sees the opposition between the 'I' and the world of what is given through outer nature. However, as distinct from the irresolvable opposition existing between thinking man and the external world, the inner dialectic between the 'I' that thinks and that which is thought, i.e. its content, has to do with an opposition over which the human being has operative power because the essence of the 'I' has the quality of thought, meaning that it has the same quality as what is thought. When he thinks about thinking, the human being experiences himself, and this experience changes him. This inner polarity – the 'I' and the content of thought on the stage of consciousness – worked at rigorously on the level of thinking could, according to Hegel, begin to answer the human need for unity between the inner and the outer world. This happens when we obtain certain flashes of insight in our thinking, as we resolve the ethical problems that are necessarily implied in the spiritual contents, thus enabling us to rise in thinking to a higher level and build a bridge towards the universal spirit. Marx ignored the spiritual quality of Hegel's argument and turned the dialectic around, focussing it on outer problems and the social conflict. He put forward the problem as an opposition and conflict between, on the one hand, the exclusively material needs of the human being – those that arise, not from the 'I', but only from the 'ego' – and, on the other, the society in which it unfolds: that is to say, the conflict of the obvious accumulation of capital within the social system. Marx saw the resolution of this conflict emerging independently of human morality, and culminating in a series of outer revolutions whose goal is the fair distribution of bread through the force of the totalitarian State. Hegel spoke, not of violent outer revolutions, but of moments of awakening which arise on the inner path of spiritual self-education, that is, on the evolutionary movement from within outwards, a path that leads us to right action. Many critics have accused Hegel of making "all cows in the night, black" by treating the outer and the inner world as the same, a picture that bears no correspondence to the real world. This critique is no more than a reflection of a crudeness of thought that has no sense for the struggle, at such a historical turning-point, to bring to an unfolding the forces of individual thinking. Let us bear in mind that Hegel was developing his ideas at the beginning of the 19th century.

Where does the need for basic things end, and appreciation for other values begin? Here we confront an individual and social problem and – forgive the repetition – something entirely free and individual which can, however, be fostered from out of the cultural life. It is in the cultivation and unfolding of his own capacities that the human being finds the joy that can be experienced in a full cultural life in which, as a consequence, this same unfolding implies the will to serve society. Appreciation of the point where the need for consumer goods ceases and there begins to be an excess of production, arises on the social level. Simplicity, stoicism, humility, the ability to save (not the same as accumulation), generosity etc.; or extravagance, outer appearance, ostentation, pride etc., are virtues or vices that cannot be imposed but arise culturally, within the process of self-education, from the depths of the soul and radiate outwards in human actions. The Kantian postulate of the categorical imperative has shown itself at the present time to be – after a few centuries' experience – a short-sighted view.

When there is corruption, it quickly becomes in social life a framework or norm through which, unfortunately, the individual is corrupted, being dependent on it for work or sheer survival. The solving of a problem by means of theft, bribery or a "contact" gives us a few examples of this; the more corruption there is, the tighter grows the vicious circle from which the only escape is through work to develop an individual consciousness that has become ethically social. There can be no doubt that, in a consumer society in which needs are roused artificially – and with no limits whatever placed on them – the only way to create a balance is through an awakening to the joy derived from an unfolding of one's own capacities on the spiritual level. This has, of course, to compete with the many temptations of the consumer world and depends to a great extent on factors of individual destiny.

Establishing the boundary between the tangible and the intangible is no doubt a problem, but that is the place which makes it possible for the surplus and its benefits to flow towards the cultural sector. It can flow both from those who find satisfaction in eating less and from those who feel nourished not only by what is tangible. But for it to be realized in practice it must be an idea that has already been circulated, recognized, understood and valued. And in its turn, the only way the intangible can come to be valued is through the influence or raying-out of culture – that is, consciousness can be awakened through individual experience, in some cases to the extreme point of demanding much creativity to compensate for the lack of means. The deepest human happiness is to be found, not in the unlimited possession of goods, but in the cultivation of capacities and in placing them in the service of others.

Starting with the economy, there has to arise on the social level the sense that, if we can appreciate the meaning of the surplus of money in the production of consumer goods, this would allow a limit to be set on over-production – on the assumption that, though he needs bread, man does not live by bread alone. In the social realm this limit involves two steps: first, to find out whether, if certain funds are tending towards use as loan regulated by the State, the conditions of production of the companies can be improved, thereby increasing the surpluses to the point where the need is exceeded for a rational production of consumer goods, and they can be diverted as a donation to culture. The second step would be to ensure that the surplus is not transformed into financial capital, through putting into place a regulation that would make it flow towards culture.

If we see finance as a corruption of the real economy within the social system, which does not belong to this sphere itself but to a fallen aspect of it which needs to be redeemed, and given the parallel we indicated between the threefold social organism and the threefold organism in the human being, one can well ask where the source lies in the realm of threefold man, of the social decline towards finance. Because the reason for the corruption of society must be found within man himself. The parallel we outlined between the realms of economy, politics and culture in society can be shown in the spheres of will, feeling and thinking, respectively, in the soul of man. We indicated briefly the level of consciousness the human being has when he unfolds these three soul-faculties. Thus, in thinking, the human being can be fully awake, that is, he can be conscious and can decide what enters his mental space – something that is not very easy without a degree of self-discipline and a suitable content, but it can be practised at certain moments of the day. Feelings stream into the soul without being fully conscious, that is to say, they appear at a certain level of semi-consciousness, just as do the many elements in the world perceived by man, although the human being tends for subjective reasons to connect his feelings more with himself, as compared to other perceptions. It is a good exercise to accept one's own feelings, although this is difficult with the negative ones, but they persist all the same and, as a goal in our development, the following question is arising: Can we learn to confront them with a certain objectivity? This semi-consciousness in the life of feeling is the same as the consciousness we have when we are dreaming. And, finally, in the sphere of the will we are not conscious; we can be aware of the motive that drives us, but in the realm of the forces that really set the will in movement, we live as though we are sound asleep. That is to say, what comes from outside, from the world, all that life confronts us with, it is hard to see as something we have ourselves produced for our own development. This is the level of unconsciousness that leads us towards an action as a response, which we can oppose if we are conscious. But the force that we experience rises up from our deepest unconscious nature, and its real power is felt in our encounter with the extremes of human passion and desire.

The level of the unconscious will in social life corresponds to the economy; satisfaction of our basic needs – food, clothing and roof over our head – is sought, in the first place, under the guidance of the primary instinct of self-preservation. The three levels of consciousness coexist in the human being, and the motivation for subsistence has a component that is instinctively unconscious. But subsistence is one thing – to eat in order to live – and living in order to eat is quite another; apart from other needs that only arise on the level of a cultivated consciousness. The economic life tends to satisfy needs that are basic and others that are not; the boundary between the two cannot be imposed from outside. This is a task that falls to the individual alone, and which he can fulfil as he unfolds his capacities in the spiritual life. The need to develop one's own spiritual capacities is quite distinct from the need to satisfy one's basic drives, and also from the ability to undertake economically profitable activities when these do not have a social content. When a person fails to grasp this difference he becomes addicted to earning and/or spending money for pure consumption's sake. When on the social-economic level prosperity grows without limit, the economy sinks to the level of finance, culminating in the degree of toxicity that signifies abstract money. But how do we explain the individual's inability to envisage needs other than the purely tangible ones? What is the aspect of the soul-life and faculties of the individual that corresponds to the realm of corrupt finance in social life?

The power of finance emerged through a gradual process during and after the cultivation of industrialism, but its exponential growth is closely bound up with the development of information technology and the rapidity of movement of numbers on the computer screen, reaching an uncontrolled level. Freed from human influence, it could not be restrained with the aim of establishing a balance. In the mad rush of technological speed the "balance" was no longer possible – as with the problem of the chicken and the egg – and also to achieve a balance in their own soul life grew increasingly difficult for human beings. Recall, for example, the fact we mentioned earlier, namely, that in 1998 – no more than 14 years ago – there did not exist what has come to be known as the market for derivative financial instruments, and there are many other statistical data which, with the speed of the computer's operation, have soon lost their validity. This example should suffice to confirm the idea of the exponential growth of finance through the medium of information technology. The technologizing of communications can disrupt the economy on the social level. The unconscious life of will on the individual level has been disrupted in direct proportion to our inability to keep up, in our thinking, with the rapid development of this communications system. It is a rebound of what has been created, which now affects and impedes the development of our own faculties.

What is the meaning of this disturbance of the unconscious will-life in the individual in relation to technology and its misuse? Before a will-impulse comes to expression in the human being, it is always mediated – to some extent, at least – by one or a number of conscious motives and, paradoxical as it may seem, the individual tries in the end to eliminate the spiritual-ethical aspect of this mediation and allow the unconscious life to prevail. This is a paradox which asks us to set aside all dogma as to how human action "must" or ought to be. But in order to heal and to repair the damage, one needs to have undergone a process of purification, because in social life it is not possible, on any account, to plead for the liberation of the instincts. This evolutionary process of purification is a long path of confrontation with evil in one's own life-experience, and it cannot be imposed by a moral or a dogmatic religious authority. Evolution clearly shows us that the Kantian categorical imperative grows continually less effective socially. In other words, the spiritual life has to do, not with repression or imposition, but with free purification – until the dichotomy between thought and action disappears, and man can act freely, out of love for the deed. To learn how, on the stage of consciousness, to observe thinking and the motives that impel us to action, is a process of self-education which requires discipline and a methodology of knowing. It is what Hegel described, in a germinal way, as the ability to think about thinking – that is, to bring a content of thought into mental focus, and to work with it. On this path one can attain the experience of unity, a flash of illumination that unites the experience of one's own 'I', active within the movement or dialectic, with the content which enables us to grasp the essential being of the world. The joy that arises as we are kindled in this blaze of the 'I' which, for an instant, is able to experience itself within the totality of the true conceptual light[20], impels us to seek still further. This activity of pure thought implies the ability to "perceive" thinking as a conscious mental activity. To train a faculty of "perception" as if it is something belonging to the outer world, comparable to sense-perception, one takes a thought, which is a still more subtle element than the substance of the arts – for example, colour in painting or sound in music. This exercise is of a will nature, because it trains the perception itself, whereby the perceptual capacity is gradually transformed, to include other levels of reality. Where so subtle an experience is concerned, it is not easy to provide oneself with

---

[20] We need to distinguish between the concept in the activity of pure thinking and representation which is a concept that re-appears automatically, without the intervention of self-observing thinking, inasmuch as what we are experiencing is bound to a former experience.

the necessary surroundings and, in addition to this, our attention is habitually and quickly diverted to the outer world. The uniting of our conscious and unconscious being is a natural process of development, and when the unconscious is not being worked upon, the instinctive life frees itself in the struggle for survival, in the certainty that evil lives in man unredeemably.

The speed that technological development impresses on the world we perceive all around us, the huge ecological imbalance that it causes, desensitizes our ability to perceive and, as a result, the faculty with which we consciously choose our thoughts becomes mechanical, and this hardens us. Since it is thinking that closes the circle of the act of cognition when it unites with perception, and given the corrupt state of perception, it is not possible to complete the circle that provides us with knowledge. The technification of the world – the very forces of electromagnetism that are wiping out the bee population in the more urbanized regions of the northern hemisphere – forces us to lead unconsciously, not an instinctive will-life of natural impulses similar to that of the animal world, but an instinctive will-life that is not merely unconscious, but mechanized to a degree that is unknown in the life of the animal in its ecological balance.

In this way we see prevailing in human society a ruthless instinct for survival, dominated by forces that are uncontrolled by human consciousness. With the advance of the evolution of consciousness there advances, as its counterpart, this relentless survival instinct. At the same time, it is accepted, on the grounds that the human being is selfish and violent by nature, finally allowing free rein to this so-called "nature", which came into being with the artificial creation of the sub-nature of technology.

The mechanization in thought, of the unconscious life of instinct which has sunk to an ultimate level of debasement – not in any way comparable to the life of the animals – is, to the individual, what finance is to the social system. Finance, a sub-product of the economic life of the threefold social order, shows itself to be in the individual life of the human being: mechanization of thinking, a consequence of the debasement of the unconscious life of will.

7. Three Kinds of Money:
Purchase/Sale, Loan and Gift Money

As we have seen, there is a moment in the development of the economic process where it reaches a limit beyond which it no longer needs to invest in the production of consumer goods, and the surplus money will have to flow in other directions. For the sake of maintaining the health of the social organism the surplus should, ideally, be used for the development of spiritual-cultural capacities. At the present time the corruption of the monetary system stems from the fact that the capital surplus is channelled towards finance – that is, to credit with interest compounded to the second or third power. At the same time there is an unnatural growth in the supply of consumer goods, and both these applications of excess capital cause sickness in society. *"The health of the money economy can only be maintained if, at the point where the limit of material consumption is reached, the surplus capital is used, not to make more money, but for the furthering of the human being with his manifold capacities, that is to say for cultural, scientific and artistic productivity."*[21] Money is not something in itself; its function is to regulate tangible or intangible values, and its use as a product in its own right brings sickness to the economy This means that when a surplus exists and one "leaves out of account" the necessary and healthy opportunity to create intangible values, the system falls ill.

In the previous chapter we saw that the channelling of the economic surplus into the game of finance is a perversion which amounts to the fall of rational man, who has created through his intelligence the entire range of goods for consumption, but who is unable to think qualitatively and is therefore debased by the mechanism of materialistic thinking – a kind of feedback action from the technological world he has created. And we saw that there are two distinct and related aspects of human and social life which, through a healthy soul-balance, enable

---

[21] Archiati, Pietro – Money is Good, Trust is Better – Chapter 6 'Compound interest is not the same as interest'.

a correct balance to be established between material needs and the unfolding of capacities.

Rudolf Steiner explained that the way to ensure that money flows to the right places in the social organism is to take away the advantage it acquires through setting itself up as a value that does not depreciate like all consumer goods. It needs, therefore, to be deprived of its permanent value: money must depreciate and expire after a given period of time, to prevent its accumulation. According to this view, there should be three kinds of money, fluctuating between the extremes of "young" money that has just been issued, and "old" money that is about to expire.

It proposes that the first type of money – that which has just been issued – should receive its value from the goods that are produced, thus making it into the money for purchase and sale, or money for acquisition – transactions in which only new money should be accepted.

When a surplus of money arises from the operations of purchase and sale and is kept for a certain time, it has to grow old, so that it needs to be used up and not accumulated. Now loan becomes an option. When money is invested through lending, we must assume that it has lost some of its value and, depending on the initiatives for which the loan is given, money will be taken on loan, that can be a little younger or older. This approach to economics would say that credit money should not be loaned for everyday consumer expenditure, but only for investment.

Finally, when money has circulated for a while – a variable which needs to be fixed in advance – and it has not been used up, it has to age still further. When it has depreciated almost completely, it has to be transformed into gift money and flow to the cultural life, where it will be spent immediately and expire. When money completes its life-cycle and expires, it has to be renewed through the issue of young purchase money, thus beginning a new cycle.

According to this model a cycle of healthy social circulation of money starts out from the excess of purchase/sale money, turns to the private or political sphere to guarantee investment in production through lending, and finally its surplus is directed to the cultural sector of the organism in the form of donation. In this way its circulation is assured and it is given an equivalence to consumer goods – comparable to the life of the human being, who first receives in his education, then produces and then rests from his labours and gives away.

When money focuses exclusively on material prosperity, this results in poverty on the material and spiritual level. *"The poverty of a fixation on money and material prosperity has the result that we possess too much money, enjoy our capacities too little, and therefore give too little support to the capacities of others. In the modern economy far too few talents are discovered and furthered. So much so that many artistic gifts are stifled. Too little trust, too little credit is granted to talents of the human beings, because we think that banknotes can provide us with a more reliable, more rewarding basis for life than the talents of human beings."*[22]

Particularly in the Anglo-Saxon countries – those who are unquestionably the bearers of the economic mission in the modern world – "time is money" is a motto for efficiency, which spurs one to action. Pietro Archiati makes an interesting reversal of this concept when he says that today's monetary system has altered its true meaning, which is precisely the opposite, namely: "The more time elapses, the less value the money should have. For time devalues all the things that money stands for."[23]

It is interesting to inquire into the significance of the symbol $. There are many theories as to its origin. One can see its connection to the caduceus or semi-caduceus – a serpent or two serpents entwined around the vertical rod. The staff of Mercury, the god of commerce, is also related to health and healing, and in this sense the money connection – the regulation of trade – also concerns the health of the social organism.

Another theme related to money – which we will not discuss in this book – is the value of land and property and the need to regulate them in the social system. Land is the only "material" that really does not perish over time, and for this reason ownership of it needs likewise to be regulated by means of dynamic ideas concerning its use, thereby also preventing the accumulation of land.

---

[22] ibid. Archiati, Pietro – Chapter 6 – 'Trust is better, when it is genuine'.
[23] ibid. Archiati, Pietro – Chapter 9 – 'Living Money. Can Money be young or old?'

8. Trust and Fear –
How are these Feelings related to Money?

In our consciousness – which, in our being on the Earth at the present time, is limited – the only thing we know with absolute certainty is that we are going to die; our life is a challenge, with a gateway that we have to pass through at its end, and this arouses fear: old age, sickness and poverty are the three evils that Siddharta discovered when he left his father's palace. Death fundamentally wipes out social differences. Intuitively we know that the only thing that can give us a generous supply of confidence to compensate for this fear, is love: *"When the night has come/And the land is dark/And the moon is the only light we'll see/No, I won't be afraid, no, I won't be afraid/Just as long as you stand, stand by me."*[24] Some artists are highly intuitive. The moon, which only reflects the light of the sun, just as our brain only reflects the reality of the world, is the only realm to which we will be able to raise ourselves at the moment of death, unless we have learnt how to enliven our thought in the radiance of thinking, through the striving to observe its original source. If we have not, the moon will not be able to reflect the light of the sun, and we will find ourselves in total darkness. Love, when it is not regarded as merely a personal emotion, but is taken up into consciousness as love for humanity, can stir our will to develop a new way of thinking. But even on the personal level, in the difficult conditions of our time and after centuries of evolution of the power of thinking, more and more people have difficulty in their search for love. This is due to the fact that there are higher expectations with regard to the communion one wishes to achieve with the other human being, as there is a readier acceptance of one's own individuality and of differences between individuals, and one therefore seeks an encounter of greater depth and sincerity than was the case in earlier generations. We are speaking here of the need to find love within a context of greater liberty, freed from external factors that tie us to obligations and conditions. There are now more and more people who intuit something

---

[24] Ben E. King – Song 'Stand by me'.

of the essence of spiritual love and who seek the path towards the transformation of the earthly love between a couple into a higher experience; while, at the same time, the difficulty involved in harmonizing these two aspects gives rise to dissatisfaction and the break-up of many relationships.

Most of us have to earn a living once we have started a family – and also before – which means entering into the struggle for existence. In the present conditions of competition – of which there are many, as a rule, presenting us with serious challenges – we experience the problem of the survival of the fittest; some with more capacities to make them winners, while others are losers, according to the parameters set by the social system. Whether we are aware of it or not, we all cry out for the love that would allow us to approach the portal of death with human dignity, and with the ability to distinguish ourselves from the animals in the struggle for existence. In them, this struggle is innate, and it is not tinged with morality; the lion that devours the deer, does it out of unconditional necessity and, moreover, out of this necessity alone. We have the intuition that among human beings this struggle has to be combined with a certain conscious, ethical element. Strictly speaking, it is always combined with an ethical element, and when this link is unconscious, life leads us, perversely enough, to be more predatory than any species of the animal kingdom. The environmental damage we have caused since the discovery of electricity at the end of the 19th century, and with increasing rapidity during the 20th century, is a worldwide concern, and more than evident where our possibility of survival is concerned. Those who do not engage with such raw determination in the struggle for existence and the survival of the fittest, are few; it is hard to find anyone who does not take part, seeing that all around us everyone is struggling, in the belief that if he does not join in the battle he could lose the abundance, or the little, that he has.

These factors lie at the basis of fear, an emotion closely bound up with the consciousness-soul that struggles at the limit of materialism to meet death with dignity. Thus, the wish to hold on to what we have, so as to be prepared for whatever the future might bring, is closely bound up with fear. *"Many people think that the most important thing in life is to possess as much money as possible, at any rate enough for a comfortable life, for a life that is to last as long as possible. There must be enough money available for anything that might happen to one – accident, illness, theft, fire, hail –, one never knows... But how much money is necessary for all this? One will never have enough money, because the things for which we might need it are unlimited. This*

74

attitude towards money gives rise, therefore, not only to insatiable striving for money as a possession, but unavoidably also to a permanent, indefinite fear that it might not be enough, all the same, whatever one has put aside."[25]

In the world today, the struggle has become so relentless that, even in those cases where material subsistence is not a problem, people continue to believe that this fear can be compensated by material security. Regrettably, it would seem that the more one possesses the more one wants, and the more fear one has for the future and for the loss of what one has accumulated. The consumer society undertakes to constantly stoke the fear for the future, for example, by selling "life insurance". Because of the rapidity of the flow of finance, those who are able to save are afraid of losing everything. In fact, this is perfectly plausible: the paradox that, the greater the wealth, the more one becomes enslaved, fits in with the idea that money is debt. To hazard a guess that the so-called "corralito" that emerged in Argentina during the crash or default of 2002 might be a hint of what could happen on a global scale, is no mere symptom of paranoia. Nor is this the case if we anticipate that when the "baby boomer" generation of the 60's and 70's reach retirement age, the social security systems and welfare states will collapse. In Germany the government is struggling to keep them going, but in Britain the conservative government is continually delivering new cuts to the – once exemplary – health and education systems, promoting a move towards the private sector.

One says that there is no limit to human needs, and this is true, in that the human being always desires more than he has, and desire is the driving force of his existence. This is corroborated by the fact that what brings the greater satisfaction is the journey towards the goal, rather than the fact of having attained what was desired. When a desire has been fulfilled or a goal attained, the human being needs new goals, and new desires surge up in him, so that he can carry on growing, and even living. But in the consumer society these desires are, unfortunately, completely one-sided and have nothing to do with the development of gifts and capacities, which also give rise to desires – in this case more healthy ones for the individual and for the environment. Fear is instilled into people on all levels of society: *"In a men's outfitter's, a customer said to the shop assistant... that he would not be buying anything for a while, because he had only 12 million dollars left, of a previous 30*

---

[25] Archiati, Pietro – Money is Good, Trust is Better – Chapter 6 – 'Trust is better, when it is genuine'.

million... Then the assistant says, 'How can someone with 12 million dollars feel that he can't buy a pair of trousers?' While she was speaking, another businessman came out of a fitting room... 'It's not that difficult to understand why these people feel poor,' he said, 'A person feels poor on the day he spends one dollar more than is coming in?'" [26]

In this connection it is clear how important it is to evaluate what the human being desires and what satisfies him in terms of quality. In the present social system, owing to restriction of the cultural sphere in its independence from the other sectors, development of capacities and of creativity with the resulting service they can render to the community is made difficult. The transition from a money-based economy to one based on the development of human capacities is an evolutionary advance which obviously involves an endurance and detachment which each individual can only demand of himself. The steps towards an economy based on the development of capacities would benefit all classes of society. The wealthier classes would be motivated to set limits to their eagerness to consume, while in the poorer classes scarcity would be compensated for by the satisfaction gained on the spiritual-cultural level. As we move towards a fairer distribution, those who possess more ought simply to be motivated by the opportunity to place limits on their wish to consume and by the unfolding of good-will in the decision to give up certain things in favour of others. As things are at present, guided by the fear that is provoked more and more explicitly by the consumer society, we human beings will continue to try to accumulate money as a security against the future, without giving or donating out of a consciousness of the path that leads across the threshold to the intangible.

The circulation of money at frenzied and breathless speeds on the world's stock exchanges, and with increased vehemence on those famous Black days which occur periodically – when after the boom the crash inevitably follows – keeps the stock exchange workers glued to their computers for days and nights on end, since they have to stay awake in spite of the zonal time differences, with no chance of a break or to take a coffee, for fear of not managing to press the right key at the strategic moment of economic stress. A tortuous "piano-playing", that brings neither pleasure nor repose. This is the perverse counterpart of the evolutionary necessity for fluidity that money bears in its essential nature, which it has now arrived at, thanks to its accumulation and its

---

[26] 'El Sábado' Magazine – El Mercurio – Santiago de Chile - 16th May 2009.

stagnation as it remains within the same restricted circles. Although we say that in the financial system money "flows".

In the wisdom of language, many of the words used in reference to money have a connection with water, as for example: cash flow, current account and liquidity; this is due to the fact that, ideally, money needs to circulate with fluidity. Water, which represents life, thanks to its fluid nature and through the mediation of the sun, raises the dead mineral substances from the earth and enriches the plants, endowing them with a form that distinguishes them fundamentally from the disintegrative quality of the mineral world. The fluidity inherent in money, the need for it to pass from hand to hand and to adapt itself – as a liquid adapts itself to any receptacle – has to take on form and adapt itself in a worthy fashion to the needs of all human beings.

The character we have given to money is a symptom of the state of our ordinary consciousness, with its ability to understand only the phenomena of the mineral world. We have to rise to higher planes as we evolve. The sequence from the densest to the most subtle – earth, water, air and fire – is a wisdom contained in various world-views of antiquity which explain the passage of the elements through the solid, liquid, airy and fiery, comparable to the mineral, vegetable, animal and human kingdoms. This is a complex system of knowledge developed by Rudolf Steiner in his 'Occult Science – an Outline'. The force of disintegration or fragmentation, and fixity or the absence of organic form is a characteristic of consciousness in our time. To rise towards the higher plane of the living world means to give organic form – through application of the conscious will – to the inner representations that arise in consciousness in an automatic and fragmented manner. "The mind is inconstant, oh Krishna, rebellious, violent, stubborn; and dominion over it is, so I believe, difficult, like dominion over the wind," Arjuna says to Krishna in the Bhagavad Gita. The consciousness immediately above ordinary consciousness, of which we can experience flashes in moments of extreme lucidity, has the character of fluidity which we have related to the watery element and the vegetable world. It opens up to us an experience of reunion with the universe, and we can move towards this by bringing to bear within our consciousness forces of thinking which oppose the atomization typical of automatic mental life. Conscious observation of fluid movement, and control of the content of our thoughts, will revitalize this life of thinking.

Fluidity or circulation is the essential quality of money since it expresses, in reality, human spiritual life, through the need we have to meet each other for the exchange of goods and capacities. In our time this circulation – dedicated exclusively to the requirements of (solid) practical life – has exceeded its limits. Thanks to the conditions provided by technology there would be, given the goodwill, more than enough to satisfy the needs of all human beings. Lack or scarcity is not a matter of quantity, but of a quality of imperviousness in the system of distribution.

In the chain of crises of recent years, the blockage in the flow of money – designed to protect the pyramid of power – seems to have caused the floodgates to burst open, resulting in an irreversible catastrophe. Despite the efforts that have been made to control the chaos (the bank rescues), the issuing of yet more money continues to provoke the same illness as before. The bursting of the floodgates draws us into servitude because of the virtual circulation, managed by unconscious human passions relating to money which, more and more, eludes their control. In view of the fact that the flow of money to those sectors which could bring health to the social organism is not raised as a possibility, and owing to the uncontrollable rapidity of its greed-impelled movement, crisis follows after crisis, and the floodgates of financial accumulation continue to burst. This is due to the overwhelming necessity, unconsciously felt, that human life should not be held back in egoism, as a symptom of retarded evolution. It would seem as though destiny is playing us a nasty trick, so that we wake up. Just like water, which – adapting itself to the forms, which cannot impede its flow – always finds the crack to seep through. The crises, with the opportunity for change which they provide, offer us a glimpse of another way of approaching things. Could this be conscious fluidity? Or, maybe, that wider segments of the world population could begin to reflect more deeply on the problems? It seems quite clear that we are moving towards a change in the architecture of money, in which the influence of the population, from its very base, is of fundamental importance. Will some groups of people emerge, who can take steps towards a new social order? Or are we heading towards a new world order centralized in a world government?

The fact that money circulates beyond the reach of our consciousness, at ever-increasing speeds in the information system, is not an achievement of man. That is to say, it is not the result of an interaction between human beings who are meeting the needs of all in a spirit of brotherhood. It has arisen through the hidden force of intangibility which money itself contains, from the time that it started to move as an abstract value and unleashed the struggle to possess it. When the opportunity to learn is granted to us, it is invariably through the suffering entailed in a crisis, both on the individual and the social level. Because the human being did not awaken to the abstract nature that money had taken on, and would not admit to the avariciousness that was breaking loose in his soul – or he admitted it, and accepted it consciously – the circulation of money was seized hold of by the mechanical media based on electricity, making it impossible for him to encompass the process with his intellect. One could say that this circulation at such a vertiginous speed was prompted by powers which, because the human being did not become conscious of them, impelled him to continue the money game at a speed over which he has less and less control, and in which the multiplication of money grows increasingly abstract. Those who are at the apex of the pyramid of power are struggling to centralize its possession, with the ultimate aim of setting up a centralized world government.

Cybernetic speed creates a cloud of electrical smog which we do not see; electricity envelops our planet. At most, we hear the hum of the computers and although the better ones are quiet and we can't hear them with our ears, the bees are affected by their electromagnetic radiation and suffer harm. Within this dynamic, money crosses a certain quantitative boundary, a threshold which, in being crossed unconsciously – a consequence of the dependency created by money as an apparent source of security – drives the human being into servitude and fear. The crises provide us with an opportunity to understand the nature of money. But under the sway of unconscious forces we are limited to the satisfaction of our bodily needs, not having been able to think of the other kind of hunger, which must be satisfied if we are to face human life with dignity.

In view of this situation, the only possible way forward is the cultivation of trust. We are not speaking of blind, irrational trust, but of the certainty that is attained through experience of man's belonging to the universe – taking into account the evolutionary process which differs from the historical process in the oriental world – and of the real bond that joins us all in harmony: *"The cure for unnecessary worry lies in the basic attitude of trust: trust in life and in all human beings. There is no doubt at all that it is easier to worry than to have trust."* [27]

---

[27] Pietro Archiati – Money is Good, Trust is Better – Chapter 6 – 'Trust is better, when it is genuine'.

The fundamental prayer of Christianity, the Lord's Prayer, consists of seven parts: the first three (hallowed be thy name, thy kingdom come, they will be done on earth as it is in heaven), a middle one which expresses the point of metamorphosis (give us this day our daily bread) in the problem of the maintaining of the earth, and the last three (forgive us our trespasses as we forgive them that trespass against us, and lead us not into temptation, but deliver us from evil). Rudolf Steiner points to the structure of seven historical epochs, using the image of the Hebrew candelabra with seven candles. Ours is the fifth post-Atlantean epoch. Of the third and fourth epochs (on the one hand the Babylonian-Hebrew-Egyptian, and on the other the Greco-Roman) we have historical records (temples and writings), while the first two epochs of the candelabra are pre-historic, meaning that we have no historical records of them. In the three historical cultures (the third, the fourth and our own), the human soul has been evolving, and with it the social system. During the course of our epoch, which began in the 15th century (the birth of the scientific consciousness in the Renaissance), to ask for one's bread ought to become a thing of the past, because now its distribution is our own responsibility.

The fifth part of the Lord's Prayer speaks of debt (trespasses), a debt to be forgiven insofar as we have access to forgiveness – a concept which needs to be raised to the intangible level of trust. A debt of money, where the latter is regarded as a means of regulating human interchange, always gives rise to moral conflict. Forgiveness of money-debt in our times is essential, and is closely related to the idea of karma between human beings. It implies the recognition by those who have more, that this possession is illicit. This is something that can be forgiven insofar as there is a change in the direction of the impulses that govern accumulation. We are dealing here with an evolutionary problem that needs to be resolved, whether this happens through man's own will towards his fellow man, or through the violence promoted by the system. This system is on the edge of collapse, and those who have woken up to the situation know that, if the right measures are not taken, destruction is inevitable, and that the remedy that is being applied (the creation of more debt) is worse than the illness.

The idea that the non-material nature of money is the expression of a debt – insofar as it is not used for noble or altruistic purposes, but only continues to be accumulated and prevented from flowing – has at the present time tremendous consequences for human life, in intangible spheres.

9. Head, Chest and Abdomen.
Culture, Politics and Economy

To gain a better understanding of the significance of money at the present moment of evolution, where the crux of the matter lies in acceptance of the turning-point where the lower 'I' of man – the ego – has to tread the path towards the ascending evolution – towards the higher 'I' – and consciously confront all the inner representations which unite him with his personal experience, and also his emotions and unconscious will-impulses, we will now present a different point of view. Initially, this point of view contradicts the assertion that thought was the last faculty that the human being has unfolded historically, because now we will state that it was the first. Please bear with me as I explain this apparent contradiction. It is possible to approach something from different – and even opposite – points of view, thanks to which it can be grasped on a deeper level. It also exercises our thinking activity, whose true essence lies in its contradictory nature.

We are told in the Bible that man was cast down onto the Earth as a consequence of the Temptation – a process referred to as the 'Fall' or expulsion from Paradise. There are two reasons to be distinguished – the first being the cause (the eating of the forbidden tree of the knowledge of good and evil); here we are speaking of something that happened, a cause in the past. The second reason for the expulsion – or, rather, it is a less well-known consequence – points towards the future, towards a cause that wishes to be anticipated in the future: so that, having eaten of this tree and learnt to distinguish between good and evil, he would not eat of the tree of life, now that he had acquired in this way the intelligence that would gradually turn into the conditions of our ordinary consciousness. The mystery refers to man as a divided being who now thinks, and therefore no longer experiences unity with the world, and perceives his nakedness. The mystery of the tree of life must not be accessible to ordinary intellectual consciousness – not until a future time when man will succeed in returning to Paradise through his own effort. To what does the mystery of the tree of life refer?

The expulsion from Paradise and the resulting confrontation with earthly conditions came about for the sake of the power of discernment. One could say that man was moving "head first" into the earthly conditions; first he was tempted and then he began to build up his cognitive nature and, with this, his intellect. The primary quality of the intellect is a weakening of the experience of the spiritual reality of the world, and its metamorphosis into the capacity to form images inwardly. Via the intellect a world of images is created in man's inner consciousness, which is not a real world but only a picture of reality, formed by the human being. He then decides in freedom – in his picture-consciousness and not in real immersion in the forces of good and evil – towards what goal he wishes to guide his actions. The capacity to form images – centred in the brain, which acts as a mirror of the universe – evolved in the course of history, and step by step the human soul was unfolding an increased capacity to understand the world by way of the intellectual images; while, parallel to this, the spirituality of the real world was losing its power in man's consciousness. The human head is a self-contained sphere in which the images that form have a limit determined by their origin, because they correspond to the person's past experiences which the intellect can store up in memory, or to a fantasy woven on the basis of these same experiences. If we consider thought in this dimension of the past alone – the source of the Kantian mental representation – we are led to the idea that there exists a limit to the power of thought in general. The transcending of this limit is the slow process that is unfolding at the present time. Can the human being weave an imagination or fantasy beyond the inner representations or concepts that have arisen from his own life-experiences? Or can he endow thought with the quality of life itself? Is this possible?

One could say that in ancient times – in the Egyptian, Babylonian and Hebrew cultures – man confronted the world for the first time with the forces related to the head, and discovered with astonishment that he was moving away from the spiritual world while, at the same time, his capacity to form images of the world intensified, and he built temples of initiation into the Mysteries. In his other soul-faculties – his feeling and will impulses – the human being of that time still lived under the guidance of the cosmos. His ability to form mental images first expresses itself in mythology. These images were more life-imbued than those that arise from our intellect today, because they were still charged with a spiritual element which the world provided him with spontaneously in his feelings and impulses of will.

In the lectures given to teachers at the founding of the first Waldorf School in 1919[28], Rudolf Steiner explained that in the human organism the head is a sphere enclosed within itself, which, geometrically speaking, is a point. The chest is a hemisphere, not enclosed completely but, with its half-moon shape supported on the physical back, opening towards the front in the direction of forces that are not at all conscious for the human being, unlike the impulses that he can formulate in his head. The ribs that are open towards the front are the physical expression of this half-moon. The upper ribs are completely closed like the head, and as the ribs descend towards the abdominal region they open wider. It is the hemisphere which supports the life of feeling, the soul-life of man, in a way that resembles semi-consciousness, or the dreaming state.

If we now descend to the third organic system, we can imagine the system of the limbs and metabolism as an infinite sphere. The arms and legs are the radii of a sphere of infinite diameter, whose centre is located at all the points of the universe to which these rays lead us. It is not a physical sphere like the point of the head, but a sphere that becomes a plane because it is infinite. Point and infinite sphere (or matrix plane) are two polar concepts that can be worked with in projective geometry, which interprets space in a dynamic way: held within the tension between the forces of gravity and levity. What we carry out when we move is not conscious for us. All that is conscious is the inner motive that provides the impulse, but not the movement itself. The movement points back to an unknown cause in the past, or to a future of consequences that are unknown to us, as this is what wells up from the depths, in contrast to the act of deciding. Whatever comes toward us as destiny in our life, is something closely bound up with us, but the connecting thread that links us to it, we are unable to establish consciously. For example, we go out for a walk because we are tired from reading, and on this walk a chance meeting – but a very important one – takes place, which we had not planned. This means that in the sphere indicated by the linear nature of our arms and legs – the seat of the human will – our consciousness is the same as that of the state of deep sleep.

As evolution advanced, a maturing took place of the capacity to form images on a mental level, and this points to the development of different aspects of the human soul. But as thinking evolves, so do we also begin to evolve in the semi-conscious regions of feeling and the

---

[28] Steiner, Rudolf – The Study of Man – Stuttgart 1919.

unconscious regions of the will-impulses; that is, an awakening begins in the other spheres.

We can trace a parallel between the stages of development of the individual and the social system which man creates as a reflection of these – the "symptom" of his evolutionary progress at any given moment of history. Human evolution as a whole is a path from man's primal unity with the cosmos towards an individualization in which the human 'I' has to manifest itself in freedom – in the knowledge of good and evil – and strive for reunion with the universe. As man grows more conscious, he has gradually to take control of his soul-faculties, which have their support in the three organic systems we have described: thinking with its support in the head, feeling in the chest region and willing in his limbs and metabolic system.

We could say that, in the first cultures mentioned here – the Egyptian, Babylonian and Hebrew – it is as though man had, to begin with, fallen "head-first" in his contact with the earth-forces. This is a fundamentally spiritual human being – still religious or cultural in the broadest sense – who begins for the first time to form images of the world which he had previously grasped without mediation of the intellect; such images are what we know as mythology. The social system arising from this is the archetype of rulership by the Gods – that is, theocracy. The image-forming capacity is still weak, and it experiences powerfully its union with the forces of the cosmos. Through the guidance of the Pharaohs and initiates, human beings receive the norms for organization of the three spheres of society. The theocracy of Egypt is a social system in which culture, politics and economy are organized as a totality by superhuman forces which are understood only by the initiates. Thus Hermes, the great initiate of the Egyptians, is regarded as priest, lawgiver and king and exercises all these functions simultaneously. *"The Greeks, pupils of the Egyptians, called him Hermes Trismegistos, or thrice great, because he was viewed as king, lawgiver and priest. This typifies an epoch in which priesthood, legislature and royalty were united in a single governing body."*[29] Man had begun to awaken to his relation to the spirituality of the world, and the initiate provides him with guidelines for the quest to restore the link to the higher world, and he can recognize them.

The second stage in the maturing of the soul corresponds to the cultures of Greece and Rome – periods in which man awakens to his own

---

[29] Schuré, Edouard – The Great Initiates – Chapter 2 – Hermes.

feelings and can think them, while at the same time he has more experience in the capacity to form images of the outer world. Thus, he is able to relate to one another two images drawn from this world, thereby inaugurating the epoch of the rational soul, which grasps the laws of nature. Steiner calls it rational or mind (Gemüt) soul, referring to two capacities. On the one hand, the greater experience in working with the images that form, and on the other an awakening of the capacity to observe feelings – also within the mental images built up in the intellect – and to relate them one to the other and to the outer world. The human being, previously aware only of his alienation from the spiritual world – i.e. of the cultural or religious problem – now awakens to conflict and to the difficulty inherent in human relations and, finally, in the organization of society. He now reaches the level of politics, as a function through which human beings relate to one another out of the need for social organization. A study of the difference between what is proposed on this level by Plato in his work 'The Republic' and by Aristotle in his 'Politics' to illustrate this evolution in thinking, would be too extensive a task. But the first, basically, in the myth of the Cave and the ideal republic, still sees the need for initiation as a guarantee of the spiritual experience – the only force that can help to ensure that men do not become corrupt in their struggle for power on earth – which raises man to a level that is higher than earthly power. Only those who have ascended the mountain from whose summit one can glimpse the origin of the shadows of the manacled men, and have descended to the plain again, are able not to be corrupted in political action, because they know from experience the existence of something higher than earthly power. Aristotle, on the other hand, points towards consciousness of the earthly realm and the laws of the intellect; he can see the corruption in man and indicates the different types of government possible and their corrupt forms (monarchy or rulership by one man and its corruption in dictatorship; aristocracy or rulership by a few and its corruption in oligarchy; and democracy or rulership by all and its corruption in demagogy; and his republican ideal). In Rome – taking the parabola as a picture of the evolutionary journey – evolution descends a step lower, reaching the turning-point, and Roman law is developed out of the need to regulate by means of an external law the relations between human beings where private property and labour are concerned. The Greco-Roman epoch corresponds to the second stage of the unfolding of thought, or the capacity to form images, with which recorded history began, and to the gradual awakening to consciousness of the human chest region, which provides rhythm between the poles and is the seat of the life of feeling. Thus, the Greek awakens to art and

85

beauty and seeks the relation of this sphere to the thought-life in the transition from mythology to philosophy.

In our own epoch which, as we said, begins in the Renaissance, the ability to form mental images intensifies for the third time and, on the level of awakening to the feelings, the second intensification takes place. And, as something new, man awakens for the first time to the third sphere of his organic forces – those that correspond to the unconscious or sleeping system of his limbs and metabolism. This level corresponds within the social system, not to the level of culture or politics, but to that of economy. His entire threefold being – his thinking, feeling and willing – is received into his individuality and the human being finds himself for the first time in possession of his three soul-faculties, thought, feeling and will, although they are at different levels of evolution: thought at the third level of awakening, feeling at the second, and the sleeping will at its first.

Let us indicate four signs of the beginning of the Renaissance which are of fundamental, germinal importance for our time and can be observed with the greatest purity in that period.

First, man will embrace the global totality of the Earth and will voyage to East and West; he will reach America on a commercial level (its existence was known of, as the Irish, the Vikings and the Chinese had already travelled there), and he will again travel to the Far East because, although Marco Polo had done so in the 13th century, the journeys had been interrupted by the outbreak of the Black Death and by the invasion of Genghis Khan in the heyday of the Knights Templar. With this invasion the global expansion of trade begins and man confronts in a new way his relation to the resources provided by the Earth – that is, he transforms himself into economic man.

Secondly, gunpowder arrives from the Orient, war loses its chivalrous character and technological violence begins.

Thirdly, printing develops, and we could say that this marks the beginning of communication by mechanical means.

And, last but not least, the nations begin to define themselves and Europe loses the character of religious unity which it had in the Middle Ages.

The awakening to the global nature of world economy is not simply a parallel phenomenon. It is the necessity that we should open ourselves up on the level where we are asleep, that is the level of the unconscious will, the gradual symptoms of which can be observed from the time of the Renaissance onwards. To raise the will to consciousness in an individualized form – its first stage of evolution – is an enormous challenge, and is illustrated perfectly in the Industrial Revolution at its height. Egocentric unity under the dominion of the lower 'I', or ego, must of necessity give way to a configuration from a higher plane, both on the level of the individual and of the social system, which, as we have seen, run parallel to and influence one another. We will now give a few examples of this necessity of evolution: the awakening to the infinite sphere on which is based the human will.

We see that, scarcely has our epoch begun, than wars of religion break out between Protestants and Catholics. The Thirty Years' War at the beginning of the 17th century will bring with it – by virtue of its outcome – the liberation of the forces of the West, whereby the ascent begins of the imperialism of the British, who are the fundamental bearers of the economic capacity in the modern world. Conflict breaks out with the radiating force of a cultural pole free of politics and economy, in Middle Europe – centres around the alchemical and Rosicrucian movement which is beginning to unfold in the Palatinate and Bohemia – at a time when the Protestant ethic does not distance itself from the contradiction of the forces of money and lending, as does the Catholic Church. But this first attempt to set up an independent cultural pole was soon destroyed by the forces of the Catholic Church and Romanism, with their wish to retain their predominance and not to make room for new spiritual needs. Finally England, through the action of the diplomatic monarch who ensures the unity of Great Britain, does not join in the conflict and is strengthened as a result. The Anglo-Saxon peoples will promote the forces of economy and commerce, but not those of a free cultural life, as the interests of its economic élites will prevail over its mission for evolution.

The economic life of today, based on technology, and inspired by its universal dominance, tries to apply Roman law in order to unite politics with culture and prevent the three spheres from becoming independent. In our time, on the level of the individual, thanks to the human being who intensifies his capacity of thinking, there arises the possibility of pure thought in the spirit of the first idealism in history (Descartes with his "I think, therefore I am", as the foundation of human existence). At the same time, man is awakening to the need to penetrate with consciousness to the level of the unconscious will, in order to imbue the ideal mental image with reality – an image that does not arise from the external world. A few centuries after the beginning of our epoch in the Renaissance, Freud was proclaiming the need to awaken to unconscious life, relating it exclusively to the sexual aspect. However, this concept would be broadened by Jung and by other traditional psychiatrists and psychologists, out of the need to introduce elements that would allow consciousness to expand onto other levels.

What in the individual man has an epistemological or ethical character, becomes social in external life; what is individual and what is social are realities which need one another for their development and strengthening. It is a necessity of our age that the human being should bring to expression his three soul-faculties through his own forces, so as to ascend to a consciousness of the universe by setting aside the personal, subjective colouring that arises from his own tastes and interests, and orienting himself within its true dimension. It follows from this, that in the social realm the three spheres should not be mixed, but should enable the human being to develop, without being caught up in the economic and political aspects with the means by which they wield power – money in the economy and elections in politics – thereby restricting his freedom of thought and imposing their conditions. The force of globalization on the economic level makes the spiritual life into a convention in favour of the interests of the lower 'I', articulated by the State as the supreme authority which is, in its turn, dominated by economic power. In the striving to make conscious his life of instinct and, eventually, to harmonize with it, without letting himself be dominated by the cerebral culture of the image devoid of content, or to transform this instinctual life if he finds the ethical content that can spur the will in this direction, the human being seeks to raise to consciousness the economic sphere, the sphere of physical needs, in order to illumine the source of his will-impulses. The struggle to overcome the instinctive character of the economic life is a mark of the consciousness-soul – that is, the region of the soul in which the image-forming capacity has advanced to a third stage. We need to develop those thoughts which enable us to grasp our relation to the universe, the thoughts that live in that part of our organism where our consciousness is still asleep, or, to use a more traditional term, unconscious.

The system of the threefold organism as represented by Steiner is not something external that can be applied schematically; it depends upon the individual and has no access to this evolution except through the free will of the human being. In this sense, what is needed as an initial step is an understanding of the evolution of our human consciousness in the course of history: the biography of mankind.

German Idealism – the culmination of consciousness-soul development – was inverted when Marxism appeared, owing to a wrong interpretation of the Hegelian dialectic, as we explained earlier. At a later date the question was made use of in politics where two systems – Communism and Capitalism – were set in mutual opposition so that, as they exhausted themselves in the struggle, the synthesis could be formed to the advantage of the élites who hold the reins of power. Marxism represents the one-sided dialectic of outer necessity, as opposed to the inner dialectic which makes possible the individual transformation of the moral forces. The true dialectical method is not something external; it is the meditative space with which the individual human being provides himself when individual and social conditions allow, with the aim of contemplating his own creative activity, which urges him on to conscious activity. The difficulty involved in this path has to do with the transition which necessarily arises, in view of the passivity with which man formerly received everything from without. In the rational soul the images which man has built up in order to understand the laws of nature come from outside – from nature itself – and this is different from the search, from within oneself, for the universal laws which cannot be drawn from the nature accessible to our senses. The moral laws are the laws of the universe, but life in society shows that they cannot be imposed dogmatically. To spur ourselves on to activity out of our own forces, and advance towards something that is completely new in evolution – an opening up to the world of the boundless universe with which we are connected through our limbs – implies an enormous qualitative change, to which we have scarcely begun to awaken.

The conscious economic life in quest of the threefold structuring of society – each sector inspired by its ideal, and specifically the economic life with its ideal of brotherhood – is a key which serves as a support in the reorientation of the lower 'I' towards the higher 'I', this being a necessity made evident by the present economic crisis. In the first place, transparency in economic processes is something for which humanity in general is crying out. The system filters out what one is allowed to know, from what one is not. The opening up of the balance sheets of the institutions with which one is connected is based on the "need to know" principle, because in one's quest for openness on the level of universal justice, opposition to such a quest is a matter of fundamental importance, and this opening up is prevented by all the means of distraction that the system can muster. This means that one should observe the sphere of social will, in order to see objectively the instincts of one's own 'I', and raise its forces into consciousness, so as to make possible their eventual transformation.

A number of authors have drawn a parallel between money in the social organism, and the blood in the human organism. If we compare the head system with the metabolic system in the human organism, we see that in the brain and central nervous system the flow of blood is minimal as compared with the metabolic system; so that we can say that suffusion with blood is a fundamental feature of the latter system. We need only compare the two archetypal organs of these systems: the grey and dry brain, and the red and blood-suffused liver. If, in the same way, we observe the cultural aspect of the social system we see that the flow towards it of money – the means of exchange for the production of material goods – is minimal, and that spiritual workers have to be recognized by material workers for the satisfaction of those needs arising from the physical body. If we imagine a small, self-supporting community, we see that there are many manual workers and perhaps one priest, one schoolmaster, one doctor and a few artists, writers and philosophers. Because the healthy development of the social system as a whole depends upon the possibility of granting growing space for the spiritual development of more and more human beings, the cultural or spiritual sector requires gift money to maintain it and enable it to fulfil its tasks. However, as we have seen, the economic system produces values that are equivalent to money and from these it can produce a surplus which, beyond a certain point, does not need to be reinvested in production – a transition stage which has been generally superseded, thus giving rise to the economy of loan. It is in this sense that money and the blood can be compared, through the need for them to flow to the whole human organism and the whole social organism. Steiner also, when he speaks of the ascent to a spiritualized perception of the world, speaks of the need to transform the human senses, bound up in ordinary consciousness with the neuro-sensory system, into senses which have an increased supply of blood, as in the child. Now, however, in a conscious way, so that we may awaken to the hidden plane of reality of which we are normally not conscious (since we fall asleep when the flow of blood increases). In the social system the State is the entity which, through its administration of money, mediates between the economic and cultural poles, that is, through the levying and redistribution of the taxes paid by the citizens. As a parallel to this, in the human organism it is the heart which assures the correct distribution of blood as between the neuro-sensory and metabolic poles. The rhythm in the administration of money and the rhythm of the heart in the blood are the centres in each sphere: that is, the political state in society as the representative of the labour of its citizens, and the human heart as the seat of the spiritualized 'I'.

In a threefold social organism the spiritual development of the individual is the ultimate aim of evolution, and only in this way does the "social contract" leave the realm of abstraction and embody a just State with its ideals of equality, brotherhood and freedom, for the furthering of evolution. Only a State with these characteristics provides the setting within which the individual can unfold his capacity for moral intuition, in such a way that this can penetrate and illumine the economic organism, instead of allowing the latter to dominate the whole system. In a certain way it could be said that the key for an opening up to the life of the universe lies in the formation of a middle sector for the fostering of human rights on the level of social equality, since it is on this level that cultural life and the economic life can metamorphose the one into the other.

Rudolf Steiner characterizes the realm of the consciousness-soul – which we are developing in our epoch – as the possibility of attaining the experience of the 'I' in the physical body; that is to say, the struggle between two extremes: the subtle and potent element that we have acquired in the sphere of the conscious life of thinking needs to be confronted with the life of instinct connected with our bodily needs. This confrontation was once based on the instinctive life of the blood in the group 'I' of primitive societies, or the reminiscence of it in tradition. But in our own time, in view of human individuation, ethics (thought that has to do with action) must arise of itself. Given the need for us to move forward to a new form in the social system, which should arise from the individual himself, it becomes obvious that, today, understanding and clarity in our handling of money – meaning man's clarity with regard to his natural needs – is a key to the transformation of the energies implicit in the life of instinct. This is the source of conflict, but to bring transparency to it makes interaction easier among people who are working together and enables them to accept the power factors involved.

In his course on 'World Economy'[30] Rudolf Steiner explains that the circuit of the economy begins with the transformation of nature into the

---

[30] Steiner, Rudolf – World Economy – August 1922 – Dornach.

actual economic pole, continues on the juridical, political or "State" level with the organization of work and leads finally to the creation of capital which, as capacity and ingenuity applied to labour, produces a surplus that truly corresponds to the spiritual pole. On another occasion he says that money is congealed spirit. The first place in the economy proper where money or transformed nature is produced, is to be found in any institution – whether of a cultural, "State" or entrepreneurial kind, and even though it may not produce commodities – because money flows to the institution by some means, be it the fees paid by parents to a college or a donation received from outside. Work has to be organized in accordance with the needs and capacities of those involved, on the basis of these resources. Finally, it will be decided what the surplus – if there is one – should be invested in, and when the surplus of money can be transformed into capital for investment in the training of those involved, or – which is the same thing – is to be used for the development of human capital.

The evolutionary requirement of our time is the release of the human soul-faculties from their natural, organic structure – that is, from the forces of what is given by nature, and even by tradition. In other words, the human being needs to bring the functioning of his faculties under the control of his 'I', and of central importance for this are the forces of a healthy human feeling which has its support in the heart. As to its social counterpart, the idea that such a membering of the threefold social system could be realized from above downwards in the macro-social system of the States is virtually impossible today, because on this level finance has largely absorbed the economy and the political sector of States, and these have absorbed the cultural sector.

'Small is Beautiful', the title of the book by Schumacher which was widely read in the 70's, offers a key to the possible advance of a threefold system within a small-scale organization of institutions which regard threefolding as their social ideal, and of individuals who wish to help in such a transformation. There is no recipe for the path towards the practical realization of what has been put forward. However, the quest for transparency in the economic processes of any institution is an important step in the building up of the conditions of trust which make possible the independent unfolding of the three sectors.

Rudolf Steiner underlined two factors in connection with the health of the social organism. The first is the so-called 'Fundamental Social Law', which says: "The health of social life is the greater, the less the individual claims for himself the proceeds of his work, and the more he gives of them to others; and the more his needs are met, not by his own labour, but by that of others." He also says that this law applies within the social organism with the same force as a natural law. The other is the so-called 'social motto', which says that "The healthy social life is when in the individual soul the strength of the community is living, and in the community there lives the virtue of the individual soul." Doubtlessly, both statements represent high ideals. Nevertheless, the difficult social conditions of our time would suggest that there is a need to put them into practice.

If we are to make a step towards the realization of either of them, an essential condition is transparency in the economic realm, as this would help to make visible the infinite sphere from which arises the individual karma of each person engaged in a working community. Without a conscious effort to view things from this perspective, no progress will be made towards a resolution of the conflict between individual and community – a fundamental evolutionary step that needs to be taken at the present time.

By way of conclusion, let us recall the old and well-known story describing what hell and heaven are like. In hell there is a huge pot full of appetizing food; all the people there are sitting around it and each one has, attached to his hand, a spoon with a very long handle. They can all fill the spoon with food, but are unable to raise it to their own mouth. This is the torment: to be hungry, have food in front of you, and not be able to feed yourself. In heaven, things are no different, but there, each one fills his long spoon and feeds someone else. This example should help us to see the extent to which the social environment we have created on Earth is something like hell; and it also illustrates how the infinite sphere which we described relates both to the economic sector in the social system and to the arms as part of the human organism – the archetype of the rays that extend towards the universe and towards other human beings. Just as a conscious awakening to the sphere of the will, through which we move our limbs, will enable us to discover that the Earth's resources are sufficient for everybody, if we learn how to share them.

It is a challenge whose difficulty Dostoyevsky had an intuition of in 'The Brothers Karamazov' when Ivan in his dialogue with Alyosha says that human beings grow more convinced of their inability to share bread with others, the more they accept the purchase of obedience with bread.

Not all the cards have yet been played in our evolution.

*

www.ingramcontent.com/pod-product-compliance
Lightning Source LLC
Chambersburg PA
CBHW022115170526
45157CB00004B/1644